EDITH STEIN

EDITH STEIN

STEIN

Thoughts on Her Life and Times

by HENRY BORDEAUX of the French Academy

translated by Donald and Idella Gallagher

The Bruce Publishing Company • Milwaukee

NIHIL OBSTAT:

JOHN F. MURPHY, S.T.D.
Censor librorum

IMPRIMATUR:

✠ WILLIAM E. COUSINS
Archbishop of Milwaukee

July 21, 1959

INTRODUCTION

Edith Stein (1891–1942) epitomizes in her life and death the glory and agony, the hope and despair of Western Europe in the twentieth century. The account of her life in Breslau and at the University of Göttingen reveals the charm of the old Germany prior to World War I, the Germany of which Edith Stein, like many Jews of her generation, felt herself so much a part. As Nora Waln says in her book, *Reaching for the Stars*, "In the realm of mind and spirit, Germany was a garden of the earth. For a hundred and fifty years the stars sang to these people." (It should be a startling lesson to us that out of this garden came horror. Each of us, as the Swiss thinker, Max Picard, has said, bears Hitler within him.)

The career of Edith Stein as a teacher and author is part of the flowering of German culture in the early days of the century. As a philosopher she made notable contributions to phenomenology of which she had learned the method from her master, Edmund Husserl. So wholehearted and brilliant a disciple had she become that Husserl considered her the one who best understood his thought. Later, as a Christian philosopher, she used the phenomenological method in an attempt to reconcile St. Thomas' thought with that of Husserl. Although the use of this method in her great work, *Kreuzeswissenschaft* (*The Science of the Cross*), has not met with universal approval, this work shed new light on the spirituality of St. John of the Cross and on the spiritual life in general.

After 1922, the year of her conversion, Edith Stein became a leader in the German Catholic movement. Her lectures and writings were very influential, particularly those on the vocation of woman. Still later she entered Carmel and gave herself up to the contemplative life as Sister Benedicta of the Cross. But her philosophical work went on. She also continued to remain in close contact with her Jewish people. After her death a picture was found in her cell on the back of which she had expressed a wish to offer her life as a sacrifice for the conversion of the Jews. Yet it is significant that she took all the measures she could to avoid arrest and death. As Henri-Irénée Marrou notes in his introduction to Elisabeth de Miribel's excellent book on Edith Stein, the proper characteristic of the martyr is not that he seeks out martyrdom as though glorying in his own strength, but that he accepts it willingly when it comes. Such was the attitude of Sister Benedicta of the Cross. As a victim of Hitler's gas chambers, she went to the death she had foreseen but not sought out, to a death as ignominious in its way as was crucifixion under the Romans, and she accepted it as her crucifixion for the sake of Christ and His people.

Edith Stein suffered her fate together with millions of other Jews. It is estimated that out of the 9,500,000 Jews living in Europe in 1939, over 6,000,000 were murdered by the Nazis. Even the bare recital of these cold figures is enough to dizzy and appall one. They cry out the anguish of millions of beings like ourselves; they echo what Jacques Maritain calls the tramplings of the Beast. Anyone who reflects upon these horrors must resolve to avoid doing or saying the slightest thing that would countenance such a monstrous evil, for the danger of recurrence is dormant but not extinct. If you call the least of these a wretched Jew, you call Christ a wretched Jew.

In reading the accounts of the atrocities perpetrated by the Nazis on their fellow men, well might one despair of humanity and of its endeavors to build a sane and decent society. But Sister Benedicta of the Cross found in the cross of Christ the lesson of hope transcending all human hopes. She stands out, as Bordeaux notes in this book, as the symbol of all the victims of persecution and war in our century and the type of all those who offered their lives to expiate the crimes committed in a Christian land gone mad.

The question has been asked (we are thinking of a devout Catholic, a Jewish convert who lost both friends and family in the holocaust) that since Edith Stein was no more remarkable in her death than millions of other innocent persons, why should she be singled out as a martyr? Yet we know that there are many saints besides those elevated to the altar, and there were doubtless many in the same group that died with Edith who were true martyrs. It is not for us to speculate as to why some who were apparently worthy have not been held up for our edification by Divine Providence; we can only ponder the special message of those who have been singled out for us.

Edith Stein is eminently a "saint" for our time, and this for several reasons. She represents all of those converts from Judaism who freely accepted martyrdom and thus became a bridge between Christians and Jews. She is the type of Christian scholar who was willing to give up the life of learning along with everything else for the sake of Christ. In the life of contemplation she reached new heights of wisdom which, later on when she was ordered to take up her philosophical work again, were reflected in her writings. As a woman she appropriately indicates the paths which the Christian woman, while remaining both genuinely feminine and truly Christian, may tread.

The book here presented in English translation has for its author a noted member of the French Academy, author of over one hundred works and long a leader in the Catholic Renascence. To appreciate Bordeaux' book on Edith Stein, one must understand what it is not, as well as what it is intended to be. It is not a biography, such as the work on Edith Stein by Sister Teresa Renata. It is not an exposition of her life and thought as is Hilda Graef's book, *The Scholar and the Cross*. It is not, finally, a *testimony* as Marrou calls Elisabeth de Miribel's work, likening it to the acts of the early Christian martyrs.

The author's intention in writing this book is designated quite precisely by the original French title, *La Vie pathétique d'Edith Stein — Méditations*. It is a series of meditations upon a life singularly poignant and deeply moving. If these reflections are looked upon superficially, they may appear to be little more than a series of unrelated digressions upon themes suggested by events in the life of Edith Stein. If they are regarded sympathetically, they appear to unfold like scenes in a modern mystery play in which Edith Stein and kindred spirits play roles fraught with symbolic meaning. Bordeaux reflects upon humility, love of family, love of one's own people, the universal love for all men, and the science of the cross as illustrated in the life of Edith Stein, and he associates with her other individuals who in an outstanding way manifest these qualities. There is Sister Valentine, Bordeaux' own sister, who immolates yet transfigures her natural love of family as did Sister Benedicta. There is the philosopher Henri Bergson who displayed the passion for the intellectual life and for the whole truth so typical of the Jewish intellectual, and who in the end, like Edith, discovered Christ. There are St. John of the Cross and St. Teresa of Avila, her masters and models in the spiritual life, who exhibit the universal love and the science of the cross of which Sister Benedicta wrote and which she practiced unto death.

It is our hope that the readers of Henry Bordeaux' book will be inspired to learn more about her intellectual achievements and to find in her holy life an example for their own. Information concerning her cause for beatification and the movement for the conversion of Jews to Catholicism may be obtained by writing to the Edith Stein Guild, 112–21 212th Street, Queens Village 29, N. Y.

In conclusion, there are acknowledgments which we make briefly but gratefully. We wish to thank Professor Victor Sampon of the Department of Modern Languages of Marquette University for his assistance in rendering the French text into

English; Father Francis Wade, S.J., Assistant Director of the Philosophy Department of Marquette University, for placing the secretarial services of Miss Esther Diehl at our disposal; Miss Diehl herself for her cheerful co-operation; and Miss Maureen Donahue for her help in compiling the selected reading list.

DONALD AND IDELLA GALLAGHER

CONTENTS

EDITH STEIN

Chapter 1

HAUNTED
BY A NAME

Edith Stein! It was five or six years ago that I came upon this name for the first time in a letter from a stranger. Following a very serious illness in which I was brought face to face with death, I was taken away from Paris to Chantilly to convalesce at the chateau of Enghien where I occupied a pavilion in the capacity of curator of the Condé Museum. It was December, 1948. The invigorating air, the woods, the lawns and gardens where I walked each day, and the radiant sun restored my strength to such an extent that I resumed work at the end of January, at which time I wrote my first article for the magazine *L'Epoque* to commemorate, although belatedly, the twenty-fifth anniversary of the death of Maurice Barrès. *L'Epoque* then requested that I do a short article every fortnight. In one of these articles, if I remember correctly, for I have not been able to find them since, I deplored the fate of Jerusalem and wondered why the Jews and the Arabs claimed it as their capital. The Jews have Tel Aviv, the Arabs have Mecca. It was natural that the cradle of the Christian religion enjoy freedom, but it was not natural that the Jews claim the city where the greatest crime against justice took place. It was the policy of the Holy See for the Levant that Jerusalem be declared free under the protection of the Allied Nations.

As a result of this article, I received a great number of letters

1

both of approval and of disapproval. One of these came from Holland bearing an illegible signature and no address. This letter brought before me without any apparent reason the name of Edith Stein, Jewess, who had been converted to Catholicism, had entered the Carmelite Order in Cologne, and who, in spite of her religious vows, had been arrested by the Gestapo and deported without anyone having been able to find out what had become of her. However, it was believed that she had been martyred and had died in exile.

Why did this letter thrust before me the blood of a martyr? I was far from being anti-semitic. Following my first book, *Ames modernes* (*Modern Souls*), there was a very fine review by Fernand Vanderem on the front page of the *Echo de Paris*, and when I, full of gratitude, went to thank him, he mentioned an article by Ernest Daudet about himself and added, "I wonder what he is driving at and where his interest lies because, after all, one seldom writes for the fun of it, except poetry or novels." After this visit was over I wondered why Fernand Vanderem had praised my book.

In my youth I had, at the risk of a quarrel, disagreed over the Dreyfus case both with Maurice Barrès who was one of my teachers and whom I admired as a demi-god, and with Charles Maurras, a friend who was scarcely two years older than I but who showed a rare doctrinal maturity. I myself was divided between the captain's innocence and the means that his coreligionists and the partisans of justice employed and which threatened to shake the social foundations of the nation.

In my middle age I considered it an honor to number among my friends Henri Bergson, Daniel Halévy, and Gustave Cohen (who was the leading spirit in the revival of the mystery plays of the Middle Ages). I dedicated the *Jeux dangereux* (*Dangerous Games*) to my colleague and friend, André Maurois, and played a part in having him named a member of the French Academy.

During the years in which I used to appear often in society

either to accompany my daughters or to meet some celebrity of literature, the arts, diplomacy, the army, or politics, I frequented a number of different circles. Among these was that of Madame Halphen who had married one of her two daughters to Baron Edouard de Rothschild and the other to the Count of Brémont d'Ars, that of Madame Guillaume Beer who had in her second marriage wed the poet Alfred Droin, and that of Madame Péreyre who had kept her beauty until an advanced age and who had given me her unpublished Memoirs which revealed that her life, in appearance so happy, had been stricken by the most tragic fate.

Recalling these friendships and pleasant social acquaintances, I was all the more revolted by Hitler's persecutions of the Jewish race. From my estate in Maupas where I spent the entire war, winter as well as summer, cultivating my land and writing my books, I had congratulated Cardinal Gerlier, Archbishop of Lyons, for having sheltered in his episcopal palace numerous Jews who were being hunted by the Gestapo. I was indignant when I learned that a convoy of Jews which had traversed Savoy in order to cross the Swiss frontier had been denounced at the last moment at the Chapelle d'Abondance, and that a German company had stopped it, for there was no longer any free zone after the debarkation of the Allies in Algeria.

But the main reason why the name of Edith Stein struck me was that my anonymous correspondent wrote that she had entered the Carmelite Order after her conversion. From my earliest years I had heard my family speak about the Carmelite Order, and from my youth I had looked upon it as a wonderful retreat.

I rather believe that no other layman has frequented a monastery of the Discalced Carmelites more than I. My father's oldest brother, Rev. Father Albert of the Holy Savior, wrote a three volume history of *The Discalced Carmelites in France* and a monograph on the Eastern Sanctuary where the Order originated. He even found favor in the eyes of Huysmans whose conversion, however, had not caused him to lavish his praise upon religious literature.

My uncle was prior of the monastery of Mount Carmel before being prior of the Paris convent. It was he who erected the chapel in the Rue de la Pompe, still very much frequented by the inhabitants of Passy, and taken over by the Spanish Carmelites after the expulsion of their French brethren. Since I reside in this neighborhood at present, I often have occasion to enter the chapel but can never do so without recalling his memory. The building of the chapel was hardly finished when the famous decrees were put into effect against the nonauthorized congregations, and such congregations were then disbanded by force. The monastery of the Carmelites at Paris was the first to be closed down. My uncle, Father Albert, was thus the first to receive the visit of the police superintendent who, before forcing the doors, came to question the prior. There followed an interrogation which achieved notoriety, as I later discovered in the newspaper accounts of the time. It seems that the police officer had asked the prior for the name of the founder of the Order, and the prior had given him the name of Elias. He then asked whether this Elias was still living. "No doubt," replied Father Albert. "Where does he live?" "No one knows exactly. . . ." Thus was Elias recalled to life. Then the doors were broken in.

A few years later I came to Paris to complete my studies in the humanities. Despite Rochefort's recounting of the expulsions and the mocking tone in which he had added, "After which each one returned home, including the religious . . . ," Father Albert, who was living as a guardian near his deserted church and his empty monastery, had succeeded in reuniting, more or less clandestinely, a small community. Since enclosure was no longer compulsory, he sometimes invited me to partake of the Sunday's modest meal, which was always accompanied by prayers and spiritual exercises. I really believe that the Brother Cook had for my benefit added to the usual allowance the beefsteak hidden beneath the boiled vegetables. Except for this frightful privilege, I was being initiated into the rule of the Carmelites even if not to all of its observances and its discipline.

But I was to come upon the memory of Father Albert once again, this time in a more venerable and sacred place, on one of those hills where breathes the Holy Spirit — on Mount Carmel itself. Not long after the first war I took with my daughter Paule, who was only eighteen years old, the same trip to the Levant that Maurice Barrès had made on the eve of the war. On Good Friday, April 14, 1922, having left Egypt and Port-Said, we cast anchor opposite Port Haifa. The fragrance of orange trees coming from the shore awakened me. This was the first call from Asia. Through the open porthole I saw at the end of a rounded cove a little town of red houses leaning against the slope of Mount Carmel. A layover of a few hours permitted us to make the pilgrimage. The old monastery rises like a fortress with its great walls, its massiveness, its aspect of strength and domination. From the drawing-room or parlor where we were admitted we could see acacias in bloom in the foreground and the blue sea beyond. The beauty and serenity of this spot are of incomparable sweetness inviting one to contemplation, to the forgetfulness of men, and to divine peace. On the other side there is a long plateau rising in solitude with its rocks and aromatic plants where one can walk without being distracted from one's dreams or interior examination. A terrace permits one to pass from one view to the other and to follow the sun's course over the entire horizon.

Meanwhile, at the announcement of our visit the prior, who was English, quickly sent us the only religious who spoke French. He was a Belgian who deplored the lack of French novitiates, when the French Fathers were formerly the most numerous in the Holy Land. I mentioned to him Father Albert who had once lived at the Carmel.

"Prior, provincial!" he exclaimed. "Writer, author of a book on the *Sanctuary* which we have in the library!"

Now he wanted to keep us at all cost and to offer us refreshments. In order to persuade me he showed me the cell with an adjoining drawing room which was reserved for the provincial and episcopal visits. There I could be lodged and my daughter in a smaller cell. By what title? Not surely as a member of the French Academy, but rather in memory of the former superior.

For a long time we roamed together on the bare plateau. He showed us the monument erected over the ossuary of Bonaparte's soldiers, who were left wounded or sick in the Orient after the siege of Saint-Jean d'Acre and who were carried in and had died at the monastery. The old land of the Crusades had not ceased to soak up French blood. The sirens of the *Lotus,* our boat which was waiting for us, tore us at last from the hospitality, the calm, and the sweetness of Mount Carmel. It was the same calm and sweetness which I had felt and even sung of many years earlier when as a child I had spent a period of convalescence lingering over the illustrations of the Bible by Gustave Doré.

Adolescence is an age of grand plans, for nothing then seems impossible to us. I had conceived a sort of epic poem in which the Ages marched along in procession with the prophets and the women of the Bible. In an old notebook I find once again a poem on the prophet Elias, dating from my eighteenth year, which appeared in a Belgian review and is dedicated as follows: "To the Rev. Father Albert of the Holy Savior, prior of the monastery of the Discalced Carmelites of Paris." It was during this period that I had, in the presence of the meager fare of that irregular community, surreptitiously eaten the hidden beefsteak in the refectory of the Rue de la Pompe. Was I hoping with this poem to pay for my portion? From the poem I shall take the few descriptive stanzas which precede my impressions of a pilgrimage and which speak the prophet's farewell to Mount Carmel before he was carried off in a fiery chariot.

The moon shone white on sleeping Mount Carmel.
Elias before abandoning its solitude
Looked up at the mountain with sadness
And climbing to the summit prayed once again.

The sky and the blue sea had the same calm,
And the silence diffused on the brow of Mount Carmel
Was so complete that one could have heard
The thin and plaintive rustle of a palm.

The prophet prayed on the rock hallowed
By his knees during the hours of vigil;
And the breeze gliding through the leaves
Brushed and caressed his lean and sun-tanned body.

He prayed, prostrating his old age upon the ground,
"Excuse me, Lord, if my soul gives way;
"At the moment of departure for triumphant heaven,
"I feel my heart trembling with joy and weakness. . . ."

All that night he spent in prayer,
Never resting his head upon the rock.
And the flowers being thirsty drank of the dew,
And the dawn shone upon the ridges of the Orient.

Then he rose to his feet on that somber mountain
And saw in the distance the awakening plain
Still damp with the morning vapors
Which made pale the sky with azure and amethyst.

And when, as the Lord God commanded,
He was about to leave the solitary hill,
He saw in the future his flourishing monastery,
And his prayers being heard, the saint smiled on Mount Carmel.

The reader must now understand why the name of Edith
Stein, heightened by the title of Carmelite, has haunted me
since Chantilly. It had, in fact, made such an impression upon
me that when I received from my sister a book entitled *Edith
Stein*,* I opened it without delay, and I said to myself: "At last
I shall know this Edith Stein whose ghost appeared to me at the
chateau of Enghien."

---

* *Edith Stein*, by a French cloistered nun. Paris: Edition du Seuil, 1954.
The second edition is signed Elisabeth de Miribel. — *Tr.*

Chapter 2

THE LIFE AND DEATH
OF EDITH STEIN

The Carmelite St. Teresa of the Child Jesus died in her bed
at the age of twenty-four under a shower of celestial roses
hiding numerous thorns. She rises in her purity and her mystical flights over a suffering France which aspires to unity and
to peace. Another Carmelite, Sister Teresa Benedicta of the
Cross, who coming from the Jewish religion to the Carmelite
Order died in a crematorium at the age of fifty, ought to rise
above a Germany which aspires to regeneration and the ex-
piation of Hitler's barbarism. Let us, before drawing some
meditative thoughts from it, look at a brief summary of her life.

Sister Teresa Benedicta of the Cross was Edith Stein's name
as a religious. "She was by predilection," writes Father René
Courtois, "a disciple of the great philosopher, Edmund Husserl,
and well known in the German intellectual world before entering the religious life. According to the testimony of Dom
Walzer, the Abbot of Beuron, she was one of the most eminent
women of our time. Her life and conversion are marvelous songs
of fidelity to the light of grace. Everything seemed to separate
her from Christianity — her childhood environment, the Jewish
education which she received, her studies under an illustrious
master whose philosophy completely captivated her lofty intelligence, the promise of a brilliant university career. Yet step by
step she was able to respond to God's call by triumphing suc-

8

cessively over each of the obstacles which separated her from Him."

She was born at Breslau, October 12, 1891, the seventh child of a prosperous Jewish family. But she was scarcely three years old when her father, who carried on an extensive timber business, died suddenly. Her mother, like the "valiant woman" of whom Scripture speaks, took over her husband's affairs, but in spite of this she did not neglect the education of her sons and daughters. Edith was brought up in the strictly observed religion of the Talmud. From her earliest days she gave evidence of exceptional intelligence. She won the highest academic distinctions and became the favorite disciple of Husserl, the great German phenomenologist. From then on she was considered in the German universities as unrivaled in philosophical studies.

Yet at this very time she was searching for some truth beyond science and philosophy, neither of which seemed to afford her satisfaction. One day in the autumn of 1921 while vacationing in Bavaria, she found in a library *The Life of St. Teresa of Avila* written by the saint herself. She tells us: "I began to read it. Immediately I was captivated and could not stop before completing it. As I closed the book, I said to myself, 'This is the truth.'"

After that Edith procured a catechism and a missal. She went to a Catholic church to hear Mass. Then she went to the rectory to see the pastor and asked him to baptize her. She was baptized on January 1, 1922. She made her First Holy Communion immediately, and from that day on the Eucharist became her daily bread. Her mother was yet to learn of her conversion.

The German university was not closed to her on account of her conversion, nor did Husserl withdraw his confidence in her. On the contrary, she undertook the task of writing a comparison between the Phenomenology of Husserl and the Philosophy of St. Thomas.

The cloistered nun who writes her biography depicts the personality of Edith Stein at that time in these words: "A lucid intelligence which is used to throw full light upon the principles of the faith in order to live up to them in their fullest implications. An ardent and delicate charity which, before inciting her to give herself completely to God, makes her afraid of increasing the responsibility of a soul by increasing its knowledge of God, for fear that this soul might slip away afterward from the light received. Her intellectual integrity and her thirst for truth cause her to penetrate more and more deeply into the mystery of God. Once truth is recognized, she adheres to it without reserve, disregarding her own personal views. She will be so *true* in her research that she will have the privilege of being able to adhere to the Divine Truth without her former philosophical conceptions diminishing the simplicity of her gift. The procedure of her thought will remain until the end methodical and rational, yet it will remain but a simple means of approach. When the time comes, Edith will still her mind, hungry for knowledge in order to listen in silence to the word of the Lord. In fact, in the face of the mystery of God she will make herself completely accessible, open and silent, like virgin soil awaiting the divine seed."

After leaving the university Edith taught German literature for eight years to the advanced classes of a girl's college in the Dominican convent at Speyer. To these aspiring young teachers she recalled in familiar yet precise language the great poets and writers, and she composed for them her little book, *St. Elizabeth of Hungary*. Before long she was to be celebrated as a lecturer and would hold an eminent place in German Catholic teaching.

During Holy Week of 1928 Edith went to the Abbey of Beuron which is situated on the shores of the Danube and which is, as Maurice Barrès says, "an outstanding place" in Catholic Germany. There she met the Father Abbot, Dom Raphael Walzer, to whom she soon confided the direction of her soul. Dom Walzer rendered her full justice when he said, "I have rarely encountered a soul gifted with nobler and more varied qualities, and in addition, with simplicity itself. Although endowed with a very masculine capacity, she had remained thoroughly feminine in her manner. She possessed great sensitivity and a true maternal tenderness which, however, she did not try to satisfy by imposing it upon others. She received authentic mystical graces, but her attitude had nothing exalted about it. She was humble with the simple, wise with the learned, but without a trace of pedantry. And I would be tempted to say that with sinners she would have made herself a sinner. . . ."

At Salzburg in 1930 Edith Stein won great recognition at the International University Week. Father Oesterreicher who attended the convention describes her thus: "Small and insignificant in stature, when she spoke she seemed to grow, as if she would take all things into her arms, the while her marvelous eyes looked into a far reality." In spite of her success she did not become vain.

At Freiburg she had the joy of seeing Husserl again. He did not appear displeased but rather happy over the conversion of his former disciple. Two years before his death he wrote to her ". . . man's life is nothing but a journey towards God. I have tried to attain the end without the help of theology, its proofs and methods. In other words, I wanted to reach God without God. I had to eliminate God from my scientific thought in order to open the way to those who do not know Him as you do, by the sure road of faith passing through the Church. . . . I am conscious of the danger that such a method entails and of the risk that I would have taken had I not felt myself deeply bound to God, and Christian in the depths of my heart. . . ."

The Ways of Silence by Edith Stein dates from about the same period. This short work, written in the form of letters addressed to the monthly bulletin of a circle of Catholic women, bears the epigraph, "If we try to contemplate in silence the road traveled by the Mother of God from the Purification to Good Friday, she herself will help us to find the ways of silence."

At this time Hitler's rule was gathering strength in Germany.

Edith Stein foresaw the decrees which would be directed against the Jews, and she was preparing herself to suffer for her people who do not acknowledge the cross of the Saviour, to pray for those of her friends who seek the true God, and "to oppose to the blasphemies of the torturers the mute supplications of her broken heart."

Upon the completion of her pilgrimage to the Abbey of Beuron, she had the firm intention of entering the Carmelite Order. She said to herself, "For twelve years I have been thinking about this," that is, since the day that she had read the life of St. Teresa of Avila and had been inspired by it, and she added, "I have become a stranger to the world. . . ."

Edith held a professorship at Münster at the time, and her spiritual director refused her permission to enter the religious life, both out of respect for her mother who would not have given her consent and because of the influence she had been exerting for some years upon Catholic intellectual life. Later, however, Dom Walzer withdrew his objection. He blessed her and blessed the painful visit she was to pay at Breslau, for she wished to see her family once again before pronouncing her vows. I shall speak later of her conversation with her mother, which is one of the most poignant episodes in her life.

Upon leaving Breslau Edith Stein went to Cologne where she was welcomed by the Carmelites. "In profound peace I cross the threshold of the Lord's house," she said. Some time later she wrote to Sister Adelgundis, "Here too we are *in via,* for Carmel is a high mountain which one must climb to the summit. But it is a great grace to be on the way, and often when I am at prayer, I think of those who would be willing to take my place. Help me to become worthy of the grace of living in the most intimate sanctuary of the church. Help me to offer myself for those who must struggle on the outside."

"Scarcely had she penetrated," says the French nun who writes her life, "by baptism and the Eucharist into the fathomless depths of the mystery of a God dying on the cross to save men, heedless if not hostile to the gift of infinite Love, than she spontaneously offered to receive this redemptive Love and to console this wounded Heart."

As a postulant she accepted any kind of work, any kind of sacrifice, but she showed a hopeless ineptitude for household duties. On Sunday, April 15, 1934, Edith Stein received the habit of the Carmelites and the name of Sister Teresa Benedicta of the Cross. Monks, professors, friends, pupils coming from everywhere brought flowers, which filled the chapel. She asked for the grace of being admitted forever into the Order of Our Lady of Mount Carmel. The provincial of the Carmelites performed the ceremony of admission, and the new Sister, arising from her knees, took a lighted candle and approached the door of the cloister. The door opened allowing one to glimpse the religious who, in their white habits covered over with black veils, stood waiting also with lighted candles. The mother prioress presented her crucifix to Edith who, kneeling down, kissed it. Then she crossed the consecrated threshold, and the heavy door closed upon her.

A few years later in the spring of 1938, on Good Friday when Sister Teresa Benedicta was pronouncing her perpetual vows, the venerable Husserl fell seriously ill. When questioned by the nurse about the terrifying vision he had had and which he had expressed in great gesticulations as though suffering from an attack of delirium, he replied with complete lucidity, "Light and shadow, many shadows and then again light." And awakening himself completely he exclaimed — and these were his last words — "I have seen something magnificent, quick, write." When the nurse approached his bed with a notebook, she discovered that he was dead. Thus the master of Edith Stein was recalled to God.

The preceding year Edith's mother had died at the age of eighty-eight after prolonged suffering. Sister Teresa Benedicta rendered her this final tribute, "The unwavering faith which sustained her entire life did not fail her at the moment of death. I believe that this faith permitted her to triumph over the torments of agony and earned for her the treasures of mercy of a Judge with whom she is now my most faithful support. May her intercession help me to reach my goal."

Edith's sister, Rosa, who had taken care of her mother but who had awaited impatiently the moment when she could come into the Catholic faith, announced her arrival at the Carmel in Cologne where she wished to be baptized. Soon afterward she too asked to become a Carmelite.

It was not long before the persecution of the Jews began to break out in Germany. On November 9, 1937, the synagogue in Cologne was burned and the Jews were plundered and hounded mercilessly throughout the city. The prioress, concerned over the safety of Sister Benedicta, began to correspond with the Carmelites at Echt in Holland. She made arrangements for Sister Benedicta to be transferred there, and her sister Rosa soon joined her.

Although she was content with prayer and the humble tasks of the religious, Edith was encouraged by the Mother Superior of the Carmelites to take up her intellectual apostolate once again. And so, in her Carmelite cell she resumed her philosophical work. Two books were completed — *Finite and Eternal Being,* and *The Science of the Cross* (an exposition of the doctrine of St. John of the Cross). The storm was raging outside as she absorbed herself in study and prayer.

The war had been let loose upon Europe and a period of persecution had begun for the monasteries at the hands of Hitler's soldiers and of the Gestapo. Therefore, the mother prioress at Echt took steps to have Edith and Rosa received into a Swiss Carmelite Convent near Fribourg. It was necessary to bring the matter before the conventual chapter and also to obtain passports. All of this required time, and perhaps the ecclesiastical authorities did not realize how important haste was. But Sister Benedicta waited calmly, as this letter which she addressed in June to the Carmelites at Cologne testifies:

"For months I have been wearing next to my heart a verse from Saint Matthew's gospel, 10:23, 'When you are pursued in this city, flee to another. In truth, I say to you that you will not have finished all the cities of Israel before the Son of Man has come.' The negotiations follow their course in Switzerland. As for me, I am so absorbed in my work on Saint John of the Cross that everything else has become indifferent to me."

She had not sought martyrdom, therefore, but she accepted it. The persecutions continued in Holland. A decree was issued ordering all Jewish children to be expelled from the schools, and prohibiting all those of Jewish origin from holding public office. The Catholic bishops, together with the synod of the Reformed Church, protested this decree in a pastoral letter which was publicly read in the churches on Sunday, July 26, 1942. In retaliation, Jews by the thousands soon found themselves torn from their adopted country, brutally separated from one another, and scattered to the various death camps.

On August 2 at about five o'clock in the afternoon Edith Stein and her sister Rosa were arrested at the Carmelite convent in Echt and led away by the Gestapo. When Sister Benedicta entered the police headquarters, she exclaimed, "Praised be Jesus Christ." Stupefied, the policemen laughed derisively.

They were taken to northern Holland, and then to a concentration camp at Westerbork. A merchant, Julius Markus, to whom the task of watching the prisoners had been entrusted and who had the good fortune to escape deportation, testifies that, "Among the prisoners who arrived at the camp on August 5, Sister Benedicta stood out from the rest by her serenity and composure. The screaming and wailing, and the state of excitement and distress among the newcomers were indescribable. Sister Benedicta went about among the women like a consoling angel, soothing some and taking care of others. Many of the mothers seemed to have fallen into a state of distraction bordering on madness. They moaned all day as in a stupor, taking no notice of their children. Sister Benedicta took care of the little ones. She washed them, combed their hair, procured food for them, and saw to their other needs. All the while she was in the camp she continued to do things for others until everyone was amazed by her charity."

The stay at Westerbork lasted from Wednesday, August 5 until the night of August 6 or 7. In the camp there were twelve hundred Catholic Jews among whom were twelve or fifteen religious. Sister Benedicta and her sister Rosa, along with a thousand of their companions, were deported the same night. She found some way of sending a message to the Carmelites at Echt which said, "I am content about everything. One cannot acquire a *scientia crucis* unless one begins by really suffering the weight of the cross. From the very beginning I have had this inner conviction and have said from the bottom of my heart, *'Ave crux, spes unica. . . .'"*

The last news was received a long time afterward by the Benedictine convent of St. Lioba in Freiburg-im-Breisgau. It bore these simple words written in pencil without any indication of their origin, "On the way to Poland, with love from Sister Teresa Benedicta."

A few years later, on February 16, 1950, the *Official Journal* of Holland published the list of deported victims who had died. The names of Edith and Rosa Stein were listed as having died on August 9, 1942. They met death in a gas chamber at Auschwitz. A witness who escaped punishment describes Sister Benedicta's attitude. "What distinguished her from the other religious was her silence. I had the impression that she was sad to the bottom of her soul but not in anguish. I do not know how to express it, but the weight of her sorrow seemed immense, crushing, so much so that it hurt her. She scarcely spoke and often looked at her sister Rosa with an indescribable expression of sadness. Without doubt, she foresaw the fate of all of them. . . . Yes, I believe that she was thinking of the suffering that awaited them, not her own — she was too calm for that; I would even say much too calm — but the suffering of the others. As I recall her seated there in the barracks, her whole attitude awakens one thought in me — that of a Virgin of Sorrows, a *Pietà* without the Christ. . . ."

But Christ was with her. Had not Sister Benedicta written to an artist who had sent her a *Pietà*: ". . . the evening of Good Friday at the foot of the Cross. The sorrow of the Mother of God is great like the sea. She is plunged into it, but it is a restrained sorrow. Firmly she presses her hand against her heart so that it will not break. Death itself appears in almost terrifying fashion on the half-opened mouth of the Saviour. But His head is turned towards His Mother as though to console her, and *the Cross is all light; the wood of the Cross has taken on the light of Christ. . . .*"?

I have borrowed these details from a life of Edith Stein written by a French cloistered nun who, upon urgent request, finally consented to sign her name to the book, a name at once glorious in the French army and in the annals of charity: Elisabeth de Miribel.* I was unable to gather any other information about this sorrowful and glorious death. . . .

---

* See note, p. 7.

Chapter 3

RECOLLECTIONS OF EDITH
STEIN FROM GERMANY

The German people and educated people from everywhere, even as far off as the Orient, including men of all religious and ethical beliefs, look upon Edith Stein as one of the greatest and most remarkable figures of this century. They see in her a religious phenomenon of extraordinary significance, a witness of the spirit of the highest order.

"She is the first Jewess to achieve notable success as a teacher of philosophy and to be awarded a university chair. Her philosophy has already been the object of study, and her complete writings in five large volumes give evidence of a scientific work that no other European woman of the twentieth century has equaled up to the present time.

"She is the first convert of this type and of Jewish origin whose holiness has already become the object of the veneration and prayers of Christians throughout the world.

"She is one of those rare educators who, when renown and glory come, take refuge in their work and their mission, and it was not until her appalling death that the profound mystery of this woman was revealed — the secret light, the extraordinary radiance of the most hidden feminine virtues.

". . . The meaning and the example of Edith Stein's life are only beginning to be felt. Future generations will have to reckon with this personality, with her honesty in seeking the truth and with her faith."

The words which I have just quoted are from the biography of Edith Stein by Mother Teresa Renata de Spiritu Sancto, Prioress of the Carmel of Mary of Peace in Cologne. This book gives many details of the life of Edith Stein the Carmelite as well as that of Edith Stein the student of philosophy who made a name for herself before her conversion and entrance into the cloister. However, I prefer to draw upon the biography of Edith Stein by Elisabeth de Miribel, since Sister Teresa Renata's book is written in German and has not been translated.*

It was through a chaplain from Blois that I came into contact with the cloistered Benedictine nun, Sister Pauline Reinach, of the convent at Ermeton-sur-Bierl in the province of Namur, Belgium. She is the sister of the famous professor Adolf Reinach who, with the philosophers Husserl and Scheler, taught at the University of Göttingen. The phenomenologist Edmund Husserl was well known throughout Germany. I would compare his influence to that of Boutroux and Bergson in France, the men who opened the door to a spiritualist philosophy before World War I, at a time when scientism and determinism had virtually monopolized the teaching of philosophy in official state positions.

Elisabeth de Miribel, quoting Edith's friend, Sister Adelgundis Jaegerschmid, who was a little younger than she, gives us a portrait of Edith at the time of her arrival in Göttingen.

"Edith Stein passed completely unnoticed among us in spite of a reputation for exceptional intelligence. She even seemed old-fashioned to us . . . always seated in the first row of the class, a small thin figure, insignificant and seemingly absorbed in the intensity of her thought. She wore her smooth dark hair parted down the middle and twisted in back in a long knot. She had an almost sickly pallor, and her large black eyes with their intense gaze appeared stern and almost distant, as though to divert

---

* This book is now in English: *Edith Stein*, by Sister Teresia de Spiritu Sancto, O.D.S. (New York: Sheed and Ward, 1952). The preface from which the quotation is taken does not appear in the English edition — *Tr.*

importunate curiosity. However, whenever anybody approached her, an indescribable sweetness lit up her eyes and a lovely smile illuminated her face, the features of which retained a little of the candor and timidity of her childhood. She cannot be said to have been beautiful or pretty, nor did she possess that feminine charm which captivates hearts from the first. But there was something incomparable in this countenance with the high forehead full of wisdom, with the childish and marvelously expressive features — a peaceful radiance which one never wearied of beholding."

From this portrait we can imagine the radiant personal attraction of Edith Stein.

Life at Göttingen was studious and frugal yet full of gaiety. The students took their meals at a small restaurant. On Wednesday and Sunday evenings, being free, they went in merry groups to Maria Spring to dance. But Edith was too serious for this. She preferred hiking. In fact, she enjoyed walking through the woods, valleys, and hills so much that she and her friends with packs on their backs devoted every Sunday to the exploration of the surrounding countryside.

She attended the courses of both Adolf Reinach and Max Scheler. Reinach liked to repeat: "One must never be afraid to go right to the heart of things, right to the ultimate reality." Of Max Scheler she wrote, "He was extremely charming, and never have I felt so closely in touch with the phenomenon of genius. His face was handsome, his blue eyes seemed to reflect the brilliance of a superior world. Nevertheless, his regular features, ravaged by life, made one think irresistibly of the portrait of Dorian Gray by Oscar Wilde. . . . His persuasive speech, sometimes dramatic, was always captivating. . . ."

She also attended the lectures of the phenomenologist, Edmund Husserl, whose favorite pupil she became. It was he who freed her from the bonds of Kantianism and turned her mind toward the perception of reality. But for Edith, who wrote at this time, "The truth alone was my only prayer," the religious influence of Scheler struck her with particular force. "I no longer recall in what year Scheler came back to the Catholic Church, but it must have been around this time, for he was filled with Christian ideas and knew how to express them with his brilliant mind and his persuasive power. His thought revealed a universe until then totally unknown to me. Though not yet leading me to the faith, it discovered for me a domain of phenomena which I could not henceforth ignore. It is not in vain that we learned to set aside all bugbears and to welcome everything without prejudice. Thus it happened that I went beyond the confines of the rationalism in which I had been reared without realizing it and found myself suddenly in the world of faith. I saw dwelling there under my own eyes persons I respected and with whom I was in daily contact. This fact merited reflection. I had not yet come to any systematic examination of the question of religion. My mind was still too absorbed by other thoughts. But I welcomed without resistance the ideas of my associates and came under their influence almost without knowing it."

She was too intelligent and too self-willed simply to yield to the influences of her environment. We must not forget that she had been reared in the Jewish religion. She could not eliminate all traces of the doctrine of the Talmud without recourse to a reflection which would be inspired by her reason as well as by her feelings.

Sister Pauline Reinach's letters disclose in part the secret of Edith's conversion. She had known Edith Stein as early as 1914 at Göttingen because the young student from Breslau had stayed at the home of Adolf Reinach and his wife Anna. Pauline was living with her brother and sister-in-law at the time. Upon the declaration of war Pauline's brother volunteered for the army and left for the front. In 1916 he became a lieutenant, and he was killed on November 16, 1917, in the Ardennes. Edith, grieved by his death, came to stay with his wife and sister for a while since they had asked her to classify the professor's manuscripts. These had been written before Reinach's conversion to Protestantism, for he had not come as far as Catholicism.

We must rely upon Elisabeth de Miribel for a complete account of the religious enlightenment of Edith Stein, but, according to Sister Pauline Reinach, it was during her stay with the Reinach family that Edith, seeking a book to read, came upon *The Life of St. Teresa of Avila* written by the saint herself. All night she eagerly read this book in which she discovered the truth. The conversion of Reinach's wife and sister was to follow close upon her own. Anna Reinach died in 1954 after a noble life and terrible sufferings. Sister Pauline Reinach who gave me these details remembers Edith Stein vividly and recalls her reply when she was asked how she had been converted: "It is a secret between God and me." As a matter of fact, the outward circumstances matter little compared with the hidden work of the soul. The story of St. Teresa's life may have been the determining cause, but Edith's mind and heart were already prepared.

I should like now to place Edith Stein's state of mind in its proper context by reconstructing the German atmosphere of her time because the conversion of this Jewish student who achieved fame as a philosopher and lecturer is in sharp contrast to the period in which Hitler wielded absolute power and imprinted his mark upon the German youth.

Three times I have traveled in Germany. My first trip, in 1905, was an artistic and literary pilgrimage along the banks of the Rhine. I could already detect a future threat, and I wondered if there were not really two distinct Germanies existing alongside each other, the one remaining faithful to the intellectual culture and metaphysical speculation formed by Leibniz and Goethe, preoccupied with pure science and art, disinterested and peace-loving; the other erected by Frederick II and Bismarck, disciplined and strong-willed, eager to dominate the world both by arms and by commerce.

After the Armistice I made my second trip, in December of 1918, in the uniform of a staff officer. During this military mission into the Rhineland and the Palatinate I expressed the opinion in a report addressed to the high command that Germany would not accept the fact of defeat and that it was necessary to draw up a skillful treaty with the purpose of dividing her, giving parts to Austria, Catholic Bavaria, and Protestant Prussia, and establishing our frontier upon the Rhine.

Finally, I visited the new Germany in February and March of 1939, before, during, and up to the day following the historic night that Czechoslovakia disappeared. I related the reason for this trip in my book, *Les étapes allemandes* (*Stages in the German Advance*), which appeared in September of 1939, the day after the declaration of war and Hitler's invasion of Poland. But this volume was seized and made into pulp when the German army occupied Paris. However, the publisher, Bernard Grasset, was finishing the publication at this very time, and I was able to save a few copies.

In March and April of 1918 I had been sent to Plessis-le-Roye and Plémont to join the 77th Division which was resisting the enemy's advance. It was my duty to draw up a report for the press. The Intelligence Office had entrusted to me various notebooks and journals of German soldiers who had been killed or captured. Most of them contained little more than complaints or longings for drinking bouts and a chance to loot. One of them attracted my attention, however. The soldier's civil status could not be ascertained. I suspected he might be a student at the University of Bonn or of Jena. His mind soared naturally to the loftiest thoughts. He was fond of music and reverie like the students of Heidelberg. He had been wounded in the leg and had fallen on the battlefield of Lassigny where he had lain in agony for several days without being discovered. I quote two or three fragments from his journal in order to give some idea of it.

". . . Exactly ten years ago I approached the altar to be confirmed and to swear eternal fidelity to my God. . . . All the time I was at home, I could meditate upon these things at my leisure, and, consequently, I have never lost my moral balance. But it has been otherwise since I left my family to go to war. It is dreadful to wander without an interior star. As for me, I cannot help thinking about the sermon I heard at my confirmation: 'Be faithful unto death and I shall give you the crown of eternal life.' I shall hold steadfast to my faith, even if, in the days to come, painful hours strike. Either I shall know how to die well in this war, or I shall return home without blemish. With the help of God I shall continue to fight the battle, and I hope to wage it to a victorious end."

The somber poetry of death, mingled with the charm of springtime and with the memories of his fiancée's love, surrounds him, urges him on and soothes him during his nocturnal marches or during his rest periods behind the lines.

At the battle of Lassigny a machine gun bullet smashed his right leg. He could no longer walk. He lost a great deal of blood. Crawling on all fours he was able to go about one thousand yards to the rear. But his comrades had withdrawn still farther back. He was exhausted and had nothing to eat or drink. On April 3 he still had the strength to write, "My strength is diminishing each day. For four days now I have been stretched out here without a living soul having come near me. However, I hope to hold out another two or three days. Hunger is gnawing at me, but my wound makes me suffer even more. I have only drunk a little dirty water from the shell holes. Now it is raining. Last night there was not a single dry thread on my whole body, but I have confidence in God. He will not let me end it all here. He wishes to make me one of His elect. For the love of my dear mother, my dear father, and Catherine, my fiancée whom I love so much, I shall support this pain. . . ."

The next day, April 4, he is still writing, "I am henceforth dead to the world and I rejoice to return to my heavenly

Father near whom I shall find once more all those whom I have loved and cherished upon earth. I will then have finished suffering, but, oh miserable one that I am, first it will be necessary to drain the bitter cup to the dregs. . . ."

Twenty years passed. Gathering together my writings of the war period for a complete edition, I found a place for the account of the battle of Plessis-le-Roye in a volume entitled *La terre de France reconquise* (*Reconquest of the Soil of France*). Rereading the journal of this noncommissioned officer on this occasion, I felt that it merited separate attention from most of the German war diaries, filled all too frequently with vulgar or insignificant material details. The man who revealed himself in this journal had kept his heart and his faith intact. Amidst the sorrow and brutality of war, his soul had become more religious, even to the point of accepting death, and his love was purified.

It then occurred to me to request some German newspaper to print the most important fragments of the journal. Perhaps they would reach the eyes of a father or mother still haunted by the memory of a son who had disappeared, or of the fiancée who had inspired such tender thoughts. Reading the story after twenty years, these dear ones would feel without doubt a rebirth of sorrow, but it would be softened by the nobility and grandeur with which the sacrifice had been made. Their loved one had preserved until the very end all of life's truest sentiments — his devotion to country, to family, to his beloved, and to God.

The *Frankfürter Zeitung*, in its issue of April 15, 1938, published the fragments from the journal. The result surpassed all my expectations. Fifteen days later I received an unexpected letter from Bremen signed August Kohlrausch. It said in substance, "The noncommissioned officer in question did not die. He was saved in a miraculous manner and is alive. I am that noncommissioned officer. . . ."

I was at once reminded of a conversation I had had with General Giraud about his escape from captivity in the war of

1914. At that time he was only the commander of the Fourth Zouave Regiment. He was to capture the Fort of Malmaison on October 22, 1917. On the eve of the attack I joined him in the *Creute de l'Aisne* where he had gathered his officers around a large map. Later, being alone with him before my departure, I asked him for the story of his first wound and his escape. Left dying at Charleroi with a bullet in his lung, he had been given hospitality at a nearby village. Since the German doctor who attended him seemed to show an interest in him, Giraud had asked the doctor whether he would be willing to forward a letter to his wife, one containing no details whatsoever, just to let her know that he was alive. The letter would even remain unsealed. The doctor refused point-blank.

"If the situation were reversed, I would do it for you," said the wounded man simply.

"Oh, yes, the gallant French!" replied the doctor.

The next day, however, the doctor handed him an envelope addressed to his own wife. "She will forward it," he said. "Put your letter inside." The wounded man put in the letter leaving it open, upon which the doctor invited him to seal it. "The letter arrived in time," recalled the general, "for although the newspapers had announced my death, my wife had refused to believe it."

The letter from the German noncommissioned officer contained, besides expressions of gratitude which embarrassed me, these words: "May he who rules my destiny and who saved me in the past so miraculously bless your life and your work in the same way!" Moreover, it contained the following information. He had been discovered on April 5 toward evening by a patrol of two French officers. While one had remained with him, the other had gone in search of the stretcher bearers, who carried him to a first-aid post. Subsequently he had been transferred to an ambulance. Owing to the length of time he had spent out on the open field, gangrene had invaded his leg and it had been necessary to amputate it above the knee. "The amputa-

tion was done with so much care that to this day I have never
suffered from it. The way I was treated in the ambulance was
especially friendly and human."

The letter ended with this request: "I have set my heart on
trying to find out, first, who the two officers were who discovered me and, secondly, who the doctor was who did the
amputation. I feel profoundly grateful to these three Frenchmen. It would be a great joy to me if it were possible to find
their names and addresses and to show them more than twenty
years later that their noble humanity remains eternally blessed."
He informed me further that he had married his Catherine
with whom he had played since childhood, and he praised my
belle action in having published fragments of his journal. If it
were a kind deed, I was now fully repaid. It was but an answer
to the gesture of the German doctor who had forwarded news
of her wounded husband to the wife of Commander Giraud.

In June, 1938, I received a visit from my "ghost." He had
taken the occasion to join a trip organized for those who had
been in the campaigns of the Argonne, Verdun, the Somme,
and the North. The publication of the journal had created
quite a stir in the German press, and I received an invitation
from the German-French Society to speak about France in
Cologne, Bremen, Hamburg, Lubeck, and Berlin. The Pact of
Munich (September, 1938), which affirmed the independence
of a dismembered Czechoslovakia had been signed and guaran-
teed by four powers — Germany, Italy, Great Britain, and
France. On December 6, 1938, an economic treaty was concluded at Paris between Von Ribbentrop of Germany and
Georges Bonnet of France.

I knew in advance that my trip could change nothing in my
knowledge of our historic past, in my complete adherence to
French honor and interests, and in my susceptibility to everything affecting our French soil. Our dead have their claim
upon us. They did not fall in such numbers in order that their
sacrifice be forgotten. Accordingly, I undertook the trip to Ger-

many in such a way as not to obtain from it the least personal benefit, and only after I had asked for and received the official permission of the Ministry of Foreign Affairs. Our consuls in Germany gave me invaluable and friendly co-operation. I experienced no embarrassment in acknowledging the courtesy of the welcome which was addressed beyond my own person to the Company* to which I belong, and still more, to the memory of our soldiers of the Marne, Verdun, and Montdidier. In spite of this tribute, however, could one pretend that the spectacle of the new Germany did not evoke in a French traveler an uneasiness which went beyond the political domain to that of thought and religion, and obliged one to consider means of defense for the protection of our country and our civilization?

I visited Cologne, Berlin, and the Hanseatic cities — Bremen (where I returned my "ghost's" visit and where I found his family united with him in respect and sympathy for France), Hamburg, and Lubeck — which were to be devastated by the American Air Force.

I had the impression that one could speak about France and Germany with men of forty or even thirty-five who had been in the war or, at least, had heard about it in their youth, but not with the young men and women who had submitted to Hitler's influence. They seemed like fanatics to me. In the preface to Les étapes allemandes (Stages in the German Advance) I wrote on September 1, 1939, "The peasants in my neighborhood are nailing above their doors the night bird which forbodes misfortune. . . . The man who reserves to himself the power of letting loose upon the world the calamity of a useless and senseless war, the man who exercises this power without hesitation in the face of his own responsibility classes himself as a monster. Nothing human dwells in his heart or mind. He is enslaved by his nervous system and touched by madness. The German people who listen to him and follow him are entering

---

* The author undoubtedly refers here to his membership in the French Academy. — Tr.

with him into a barbarity which knows nothing but force."

I had met Saint-Exupéry at Berlin. He was a tall, stout man
of about forty with large shoulders and a powerful chest, a
square, good-tempered, peaceful, and serious face with beautiful eyes accustomed to seeing at great distances, a large flat
nose, a thin mouth, the look of a lord and a peasant at the
same time. I had admired his *Wind Sand and Stars* which I
had the joy of introducing to the French Academy and which
had been awarded the grand prize for novels.

We went together to visit Crossinsee three hundred kilometers
from Berlin. Crossinsee was one of the three German schools
where the chiefs of the nation were educated, the leaders of
the people, the little fuehrers under the big Fuehrer. After
visiting this laboratory of the will, we were taken into the library
where we saw shelves loaded with history, geography, sociology,
and biology books. "Are the pupils," we asked, "permitted to
read books of a different point of view, for example, the works
of Marx or Auguste Comte?" "Certainly they are free," we
were told. "And what if they have objections to National
Socialism?" "They voice them and they are refuted." "And if
the refutation does not appear convincing to them?" "They are
dismissed." With a smile the director who was showing us
around added, "That never happens. Our dogma is the German Man." And consequently, German superiority over all
peoples. From here it is but one step to domination.

I remember this conversation and the thoughts exchanged
with Saint-Exupéry during our return trip. We both left Germany in haste after the brutal absorption of Czechoslovakia,
for we believed that war was close. We returned to France not
without misgivings, for we had seen on the spot the increase
in armaments and the development of German morale, and we
knew (Saint-Exupéry especially in regard to his own specialty,
aviation) the lack of adequate preparations in France.

Today Germany has been conquered, but she is once again
rising from amidst the ruins. In spite of the memory of German

crimes, there are things that give me hope that Germany will enter into the European Alliance against barbarian invasion. There is the example of that noncommissioned officer who fought in World War I with a mind free of hatred. There are the various books and articles which I consulted, like those of Count Robert d'Harcourt whose family, however, suffered cruelly. There is the work of Mme. Yvonne Pagnez, a former prisoner of the Gestapo in Berlin, who expressed her gratitude to the Catholic priests and Protestant ministers who had helped her to escape, and to the judge of Constance who had aided her in her flight into Switzerland. There are the memoirs of Anna Reicht, the aviatrix who gave herself completely but chivalrously to the service of her country. But above all, it is the example of Edith Stein which, if it were understood, and if she were to be canonized by the Catholic Church, could stir the German soul to its depths by fostering a kind of reflection which would exclude every racial idea and every idea of vengeance against the Allies.

A German writer, Paul C. Berger, does not hesitate to affirm that Hitler believed the primary function of the people living in the heart of Europe to be to protect it against invasion from the east. But why then attack France and England? Why did Hitler trample on Poland and the Ukraine instead of making allies of them? Why did he instill in the German youth such dreadful pride? And why did he wish to make of them supermen superior to all nations through the use of sterilization which prevents the reproduction of the sick and the weak, and by the persecution of the Jews which would do away with musicians like Mendelssohn, poets like Heinrich Heine, scientists and philosophers like Einstein?

There have been other men more prudent of judgment and broader in intellectual vision — a saint and a man of genius — who envisaged the struggle differently from what Hitler did. St. Louis wanted to reunite all Christendom against the Tartars after concluding peace with England, a move which would have prevented the Hundred Years' War that drained away the energy of two nations. Napoleon assembled the Grand Army composed of all the peoples of the European continent against Russia and marched as far as Moscow.

"Certainly," I wrote in the preface to *Les étapes allemandes* on September 2, 1939, "there are still in Germany noble souls who are distressed by the advent of Hitler, like the one I brought to light in my story devoted to the 'ghost' of the war. Nevertheless, let there be no mistake about it, Hitler must not be separated from a country nor from a race which, historically, has too often disturbed European equilibrium. He is its popular emanation, lacking even the aristocracy of a Bismarck. . . ."

In face of the imminence of war I identified the German nation too closely with its dictator who held it by force through the army and the police. The army plotted against him, and the nation through accumulated disasters finally regained possession of itself. The glorification of Edith Stein, acknowledged in her canonization by the Church, would have to be one of the evident causes of German resurrection.

Chapter 4

HER
HUMILITY

From the combined accounts of her family, friends, professors, pupils, and her Carmelite Sisters we are able to reconstruct the physical appearance and the personality of Edith Stein. She was not pretty, but she was liked immediately. Her face was round, her nose somewhat wide, her hair parted in the middle above her high forehead, her chin well molded and her eyes sparkling with intelligence. She did not try to please, but she was pleasing all the same with her modest manner, her neat and plain attire, her arms full of books or carrying a briefcase, and her simplicity devoid of all artifice. In a word, she was *true*. Those around her felt it instinctively and respected her. She achieved success in her studies, in her writing, in her teaching and lectures, and at the conventions, yet never did she evidence the least vanity over it.

From the moment that Edith set her foot upon the path which was to lead her to Carmel she was absorbed by something which went beyond the human confines of self-respect and pride. After she had entered the Carmelites, her superiors had to order her to take up once again her habitual studies and her philosophical and religious works, for she had willingly sacrificed her literary renown and was content to be a Sister like the others, sharing with them their daily tasks. Blessed be those superiors who understand that the cloister does not put an end to genius. Fra Angelico enclosed in his Franciscan monastery at Florence made use of the liberty which was permitted him to paint his frescoes in praise of God and of the Blessed Virgin. So Edith Stein in her cell, far from the clamor of the world and from the Jewish persecutions which were then raging outside, wrote her books, *Finite and Eternal Being* and *The Science of the Cross*.

In truth, Edith Stein ought to serve as a model for all writers and artists because of her generous and benevolent humility. She prepared her courses, her lectures, and her writings without ever thinking of herself. She willingly deprived herself of human love, for she was inspired only by the love of truth in which was hidden the love of God, Who finally appeared to her in all His splendor. She lived in an intense faith. At first she did not know what it was she was seeking in her youthful enthusiasm, but in her purity and her charity she was certain that she would discover it. Then she caught a glimpse of the dawn, as she was coming out of the night in which she had struggled with a philosophy which did not satisfy her. At last she stretched forth her arms, for she had suddenly discovered Jesus on the cross whom St. Teresa of Avila had revealed to her.

In every age poets, prose writers, painters, sculptors, and musicians have displayed their worth and their pride. Exception must be made for a few — among them the greatest geniuses — and especially for the architects, those master builders who built the cathedrals and whose names we do not know. At the time of the controversy over *The Cid*, Pierre Corneille proclaimed, "I know what I am worth, and I believe what they say about me." But that was Corneille, whereas Molière as model for his Trissotin and his Vadius had all too many to choose from among the vain and forgotten authors of the seventeenth century, and the same can be said for the sonnet of Oronte. The fashion of vanity among writers and artists is in no danger of disappearing. I shall cite two examples of it, both taken from abroad, one of a writer of genius, the other of a renowned novelist, both deceased: Gabriele d'Annunzio and Mathilde Serao.

My first visit with Gabriele d'Annunzio, which took place at the Cathedral of Notre Dame in Paris, has remained in my memory, for it was quite unusual. Pitiless creditors had compelled the author of *The Child of Pleasure* to sell his books, his paintings, and his house. He had fled in disgust and had taken refuge in France, staying part of the time on the Avenue Kléber in Paris among his admirers, especially his feminine ones, and the rest of the time at Arcachon among the pine woods and in the vicinity of the sea.

Now, a gracious lady, who was a lover of music and a pupil of Vierne (the famous blind organist who was to die at his work as he played his *Cantata*), had invited me in great mystery to an organ recital at Notre Dame at six o'clock in the evening. What was going to happen there?

At six o'clock — it was in the month of May when the days grow longer — I entered the cathedral. It was the time of day that the author of *The Flame of Life* called the hour of Titian. Triumphing for an instant over the clouds, the sun penetrated the central nave through the big rose window, but it did not succeed in conquering the immense nave. The shade already occupied entire areas of the transept and apse and wandered under the arches, apprehensive of this return of light after a foggy afternoon. Fearful, it came and went, losing and regaining its sway.

What the sun had not been able to do, the organ accomplished. It filled the entire cathedral. The power and joy of Bach, the proud and sad nobility of César Franck descended upon it. The three naves were no longer empty. Insensible to the struggle between light and shadow, they seemed to listen.

Such was the oratorio to which I had been summoned. Gabriele d'Annunzio had managed to have the organ of Notre Dame opened so that we might hear the fugues of Bach while the setting sun made its way through the big rose window. He had blended the harmony of the vaults with that of light and sound. When I finally came into his presence, I saw a small, slightly stooped man with a sharp, pointed face lengthened by a short beard confined to the chin, small slits of eyes, a feline and mephistophelian smile, and thin, determined lips. The total effect was odd, irritating — and unforgettable. He must have exercised a sort of magical charm to judge from the retinue of beautiful women who accompanied him.

"Have you ever before heard an organ at this hour? The evening is the hour for the organ," he said.

A passage from *The Flame of Life* leaped into my mind. "Do you feel autumn, Perdita?" "Yes, within me." "Did you not see it yesterday when it descended upon the city?" However, I formulated, somehow or other, a sentence in which I expressed my admiration for him as a novelist.

"Yes," he agreed, "but I am still a much greater poet."

That was true. The author of *Lauds* and of *Nocturns* was a great poet. But he discouraged enthusiasm, so superior was his own.

I related the story of this scene at Notre Dame, except, of course, for the dialogue, in an article which I wrote at that time for *Figaro*. The result, which I had not foreseen, was the closing of the cathedral to these lovers of art. D'Annunzio had come there under false pretenses at that magical hour.

My second example is taken from a conversation (at which I was present as a mute participant) between Paul Bourget and Mathilde Serao, the author of the famous novel, *The Land of Cockayne,* in which the characters are the tenants of a large house in Naples but in which the house itself is the principal character. When Paul Bourget told Mathilde that she possessed genius, she replied:

"No, my dear, I do not have genius, only an *immense* talent." This reply portrays her completely.

Both of these great Italians, although of unequal stature,

showed forth in their vanity a childish naïveté which lends itself to jest. But men of letters in France, as well as elsewhere, display in broad daylight their congenital pride, and I myself am not exempt from it when I cite the replies of Gabriele d'Annunzio and Mathilde Serao. A number of writers, even Catholic writers who ought to practice one of the greatest of the Christian virtues, humility — the humility of which Edith Stein gives us such an astonishing example — do not hide their feelings enough, and do not always succeed in concealing the high opinion which, rightly or wrongly, they have of themselves and which they would like to impose upon everyone else. "Pride," says one of Tchekhov's characters in *The Cherry Orchard*, "is only the religion of oneself." In contrast to this I choose three masters — Bourget, Barrès, and Bergson — in order to show the heights they reached in the attainment of honor.

Paul Bourget's conversion manifested itself in the Christian virtues which little by little pervaded him. He had been converted through the influence of his wife, who was a pious person and extraordinarily learned in everything which concerned religion, and also through the influence of his research into the causes of human life.

There are two ways of demonstrating the superiority of Catholicism. One rests upon the divinity of Jesus Christ and upon the superhuman perfection of His teaching. Such proofs are intrinsic. The other, instead of facing the problem directly, approaches it in a roundabout way, and since a tree is judged by its fruit, gathers the fruit of the tree instead of watching it grow in the light. If Catholicism, says this approach, is not satisfied with fortifying our inner life and with sustaining us in our trials, but is, moreover, the best agent, the best guarantee of our happiness, either from the personal or from the general point of view, if it is found to solve all difficulties of both individual and social life, is not its truth then proved? Are the facts in favor of Catholicism or against it? That is the whole question.

It was in this way that Paul Bourget was able to link all of his novels to the same guiding principle and to bring harmony into the development of his work. With his first novels he began an inquiry into society and conducted it with a completely scientific method. However, he undertook this inquiry for the sake of observation and analysis without seeking to draw any conclusions from it. Thus, his first novels complacently portrayed the evil of the passions — complacently, that is, without any doubt about their attractiveness, but also lucidly, that is, without hiding anything of their consequences. And what were these consequences? The debasement, the degradation of souls. These novels were, therefore, indictments against passion, but indictments singularly acquainted with the resources and the tricks of the enemy and, at times, as appealing as pleas.

However, Paul Bourget was right in maintaining that there was no cleavage between the first part of his work and the last. There would have been a cleavage had he written novels in the style of the Romantics, extolling and exalting passion, giving it every right and praising it even in its consequences. There would have been a cleavage had he written novels extolling and exalting pleasure, as was done in the eighteenth century, or sensuality, as is the fashion today. As he dissected, dispassionately and without partiality, the life of his age, he would have contradicted his present doctrine (that is, except for his manner of exposition) only if at the end of his analysis he had arrived at different facts, that is to say, facts revealing a weakness in Catholic morals.

After becoming a Catholic, Paul Bourget did not change anything in his method of writing novels. He continued to analyze minutely situations borrowed from contemporary life or directly inspired by it. But inasmuch as he knew what the fatal conclusion of his analysis would be, he was no longer satisfied to let the facts speak for themselves for want of knowing how to interpret them. He commented upon them, explained them, and eloquently made plain to us their consequences.

What is a singular and infinitely rare thing is that he himself corrected his early novels in order to eliminate the scenes in which he had allowed the passions of the flesh to speak too freely. But he wrote, "There is a sentence of Pascal which dominated my thought for a long time: 'in order that a religion be true, it must have known nature.' The whole effort in all of my work has been to try to establish that a scientific knowledge of human life issues from laws which are precisely those of the Church. I have done nothing more than to repeat the thesis held by Balzac in his preface to *The Human Comedy*, and it surprises me that Catholic writers have not brought it to light again."

Bourget's old age was overwhelmed with both moral affliction and physical ailments. He suffered the grief of losing his wife even before her death, for she went out of her mind. The depressing weight of sickness which necessitated long periods in the hospital caused him to suffer much agony and finally to die in humiliation. These bitter experiences had led him to make severe judgments on contemporary literature. But shortly before his death he became more tolerant, and he prayed constantly. He lived on until Christmas morning — this man who had worked so often in the presence of the fresco of Luini which adorned his study and in which he could see, in the poverty of the stable, the Virgin holding up the Child Jesus so that the Magi might adore Him. He died on the dawn of the Nativity — this man who had so much desired to live on in the *terrestrial immortality* of the family, to use the expression of Taine, his venerated master. He died while the bells were saluting the birth of a Child.

It was two-thirty in the morning. In his hands he held a crucifix while the women around him prayed. From the street came the sound of singing. Were some happy party-goers returning home? But suddenly the singing ceased as though cut short by some invisible command.

It was indeed an invisible command. From the line of automobiles assembled outside of a neighboring hotel where people were celebrating Christmas the chauffeurs had gathered around one of them who knew. "In that house," he told them, "Paul Bourget is dying. There must not be any noise."

This was the last echo of human glory, and the chauffeur began to relate to his attentive companions the story of *Lazarine*, which he had read. He spoke in a low voice. When the celebrators came out singing joyfully, the chauffeur quieted them, and they went away down the street without noise. But the men, as they passed the house of mourning, tipped their hats, and the women made the sign of the cross. This was the last episode in a life which, after the pealing of the bells, came to an end in silence.

Maurice Barrès had gone through ambition and pride. The war changed him, but even before the war he showed signs of this change. As proof of this I need only mention his reply to Jaurès who, *à propos* of a suicide of a high school boy from Clermont in 1909, attacked Catholic doctrine. Barrès made precise his position with regard to the Church.

"Gentlemen," he said, "about twenty years ago, when I was a member of Parliament, I met Mr. Brunetière and I asked him, 'why are you not interested in becoming a member of parliament?' He replied: 'Concerning religious matters, in which I am passionately interested, they could put to me questions which for the moment I am not disposed to answer.' Well, as for me, I have no such difficulty. It would greatly diminish my authority, whatever it be, in these important questions if I did not affirm clearly my own intellectual position. I am one of those who has substituted the pursuit of laws for the pursuit of causes. My knowledge of history, incomplete though it be, and my own experience of existence have taught me that the laws of life and the laws of health for nations, as well as for individuals, are in harmony with the decalogue that the Church brings us. Furthermore, I see in Catholicism the atmosphere in which all of the magnanimity and the sentiments of our race develop most naturally. And thus it was that a few weeks ago when I was visiting Rouen I felt there with the utmost vividness that it was not at Burgos nor on the roads of Andalusia that *The Cid* was born, but in the shadow of the churches of Normandy. Social sanity and the exaltation of the highest powers of the soul — that is the double virtue that I find in Catholicism. That is what it begets, and that is why I defend it with filial respect."

Shortly before his death Barrès wrote in the *Echo of Paris,* "This is the law: those who are most in view are the least noticed. Those who are best known are nobodies. They are judged by their caricature. . . . Their enemies have only to put masks on them in order to have the right to detest them. . . ."

From the beginning of his career he was a great fighter, and he remained so for a long time. His contempt descended from on high. His mere presence in the Chamber of Deputies disturbed the popular renown of those politicians who have patronage but no message. He liked the combative spirit of journalism. He knew how to hate, to tear, and to devour. What controversialist has exceeded in relentless precision and insolent scorn the pages of *Their Faces* or of *The Cesspool?* Nevertheless, on the day of mobilization in 1914 he gave up being a polemicist and sought only to unite all Frenchmen in the common goal of saving their country. It was the war which brought him peace. All he wanted to do was to bring about unity among the various intellectual groups of France. And when the war was over, he did not take up the fight again but attempted to act through other means. There was hardly any curiosity left in him now. His only purpose was to discover the flame, "the mystic spark through which everything that is religious, poetic, and inventive in the world appears."

This flame he sought in Asia in his *Inquiry into the Countries of the Levant.* He sought it around him in our country. He sought it within himself. His *Notebooks* bear the burning testimony of this. In front of me I have his *XIIth Notebook.* Three pages at the end are devoted to the Child Jesus in the midst of the doctors, confronting with His natural and supernatural candor their presumptuous intellectualism. It reminds me of the drawing of Ingres in the Museum of Montauban, far superior to the oil painting which is a transposition of it. The Infant God by Ingres rivals that of Da Vinci in the Ambrosian Library at Milan, and the Infant God of Barrès rivals the Joas of Racine's *Athalie*.

On December 9, 1923 I attended the ceremony at Charmes where Barrès, as he had desired, was buried in the family vault. The small church to which he often went on Sundays was decorated with lights and flags in order to do him honor. It was filled to capacity, and it was in an atmosphere of fervor that the liturgical songs were sung. When the Office of the Dead was over, a voice spoke out to bring him the loving farewell of the Church. It was the former pastor of Charmes, today bishop of Saint-Dié, and he wished to recall something that had not been said at the time of the national funeral at Notre Dame, namely, that this apologist from the outside, who had not penetrated into the inner organism of religion, was the faithful friend and valuable defender of the Church. Had he not in hearts like his own, thirsty for eternity, opened the eternal fountains?

He ended his life above ambition and pride in the search for truth which is very close to humility.

Henri Bergson had, through his philosophical mind which sought nothing but the exact truth, been preserved from ambition and pride in spite of the many beautiful women who used to come to hear his lectures at the College of France. The last time I saw him was at Aix-les-Bains where he had come because of his rheumatism at the end of the month of August in 1939, a few days before the declaration of war. This old man of eighty, by sheer will power, had for fifteen years triumphed over a disease which seemed to have marked him for its victim. His limbs were threatened with paralysis, and his muscles refused to function.

Does man, then, have the power to turn back sickness and

death? Did not Goethe say that we only die because of the infirmity of our will? And did not Gabriele d'Annunzio, speaking to me of the premature death of Maurice Barrès, explain it as a moment of distraction? I was in the presence of one of the most beautiful examples of human courage, a courage which did not falter even once in fifteen years.

Before this visit I had reread Bergson's *The Two Sources of Morality and Religion,* and from it I remembered these words, "A decision is imperative. Humanity groans, half-crushed under the weight of its own progress. It does not sufficiently realize that its future lies in its own hands. Man's first task is to decide whether or not he wishes to go on living. Then he must decide whether he wants merely to live or to put forth the extra effort required for fulfilling, even on our refractory planet, the essential function of the universe which is a machine for the making of gods."

The nature that Jean-Jacques extolled offers only a picture of war. Peace is solely the work of the intelligence. The duty placed upon humanity by Bergson is the return to the divine that Renan had already recommended. And if this return to the divine does not go far enough to reach the one, efficacious God, then it only multiplies the approaches to Him. How far has humanity advanced? That was the question that I was burning to ask him. But he avoided it, instead confessing to me his aversion for Hitler who prevented him from working.

"I can no longer give myself to reflection in the state of uncertainty in which we find ourselves. The shadow of Hitler spreads over the world. He will not permit thought to follow serene paths. Everything we love is today threatened. Is Germany returning to paganism and to the gods of the forest? Is she forgetting everything that humanity has conquered in the disinterested domain of the intelligence? Has humanity progressed only to destroy itself, and has its progress been limited to mechanical inventions and to the instruments of death? I cannot detach my mind from this intellectual affliction nor isolate myself from the danger which hovers over the world and over my country. However, I do not at all doubt that, if the conflagration of the nations cannot be avoided, it will end in the crushing of this Germany which, under Hitler's yoke, has made Force its idol. . . ."

Before leaving, I took one last look at this admirable, little old man who had robbed his body from paralysis and freed his soul from the materialistic errors which are dragging humanity to its doom.

How far did he go in the search for the truth? Jacques Chevalier, his disciple, tells us that in his last moments he not only recognized the one God, but the God-Man, Jesus the Redeemer, and that he wished to die in the Catholic faith. Does not baptism of desire suffice?

He would have bowed low upon learning of the conversion of Edith Stein, and he would have admired her philosophical writings which come to the conclusion of religious humility and submission to God. For she entered into *The Ways of Silence* and had no pride of any sort. When her superiors ordered her to take up her pen again, she accepted, not joyously but out of obedience.

She admits having committed one single fault when, torn from her convent by the Gestapo, she entered the police station and cried out, "Praised be Jesus Christ!" This was the only cry she made to call martyrdom upon herself. She knew very well that martyrdom was at the end of her deportation. She had no illusions. She looked with disconsolate sadness at her sister Rosa, who still hoped. But her last act of humility, the greatest, the most passionately moving was that as long as she could, she avoided martyrdom. She quoted the Gospel of St. Matthew, "When you are pursued in this city, flee to another. . . ." She sought a passport so that she might transfer from the Carmelites at Echt in Holland to the Carmelites at Fribourg in Switzerland. Alas! The ecclesiastical authorities were not in enough of a hurry. . . . As a prisoner she prepared herself in silence for the visitor who opens the doors of eternal life. And this deathly visitor invited her to the crematory oven.

Thus, she is above all an example of humility, but a humility which borders upon the greatest generosity, for it contains the absolute gift of herself without reservation to God.

Chapter 5

HER LOVE FOR
HER FAMILY

Everyone knows Napoleon III's reply to the insult of Prince Jerome. "Actually, you have nothing of the Emperor Napoleon," Prince Jerome had said. "Oh yes," replied Napoleon III, "I have his family. . . ." As a matter of fact, the Bonaparte clan, greedy and never sated, had circumvented the emperor, snatching prebends and kingdoms, or at least principalities, from him, and Napoleon, instead of breaking the family chains had remained shackled by them.

Napoleon III's rejoinder reminds me of a remark by George Moore, the great English critic, with whom I was invited to dine at the British Embassy. When I was introduced to him, he said to me, not without irony, "Ah! You are the one who is the novelist of the family! Well, the best thing is to quarrel with it once and for all the first time it is reunited. That is the only way to have peace and to avoid being poisoned by it. . . ."

This is a paradox that preoccupies contemporary man, to judge from our literature in which, to say the least, the family appears in a bad light. Most of the novels of the present day depict fathers and mothers unfavorably and represent the children as wanting to lead their own lives, revolting against the preceding generation which tries to impose its tastes, ideas, and feelings upon them.

In the last audience that His Holiness Pope Pius XII was

she had taken up from the lifeless hands of her husband, personally attended to Edith's bringing up, especially her religious education. She took her regularly to the ceremonies of the synagogue. How was it that she did not realize the path that her daughter was to follow? For Edith was marching, even hastening toward the truth, and the truth was none other than Jesus Crucified, God made Man. She asked for baptism which opened up to her the Christian life. But it remained for her to tell her mother of her conversion. Here I will let her biographer, Elisabeth de Miribel, tell the story.

"This news entailed the risk of striking at the heart of her old mother, of damaging a marvelous intimacy made up of mutual tenderness and confidence. It entailed the risk of creating an abyss of misunderstanding between mother and daughter. What was to be done? Edith did not consider using the roundabout way of an explanatory letter. She went directly to the point. She left for Breslau and went to the family residence, and there, kneeling down before her mother and looking straight into her eyes, she murmured softly but firmly, 'Mama, I have become a Catholic.'

"Then this heroic mother who year after year had borne up nobly in all sorts of trials, managing at the same time the rearing of seven children and the directing of her business, this valiant woman broke down and wept.

"Edith did not expect this, for never had she seen her mother weep. She had foreseen reproaches, violence, a break. But her mother wept, and soon the tears of Edith mingled with hers. In this moment two generous beings strongly united by the ties of the flesh realized that they were coming to a crossroad. From then on the ways of their lives would take diametrically opposite directions. Each one in her own way would find in her respective faith the courage to offer to God the sacrifices called for.

"A Catholic friend of the Stein family, a witness of the effect produced by Edith's conversion upon her family, makes this comment: 'I am convinced that the transformation wrought by grace in Edith, the supernatural force which animated her, dis-armed Mrs. Stein. This God-fearing woman, without under-standing it, sensed that her daughter was immersed in the mystery of divine grace. In spite of her extreme affliction, she bowed before this mystery, acknowledging herself beaten and powerless. From the first meeting all her friends could notice that Edith was a changed person, although she clung to her family with as much love as ever and did everything she could to prevent any change in their relationships.' "

Her brothers and sisters accepted her conversion, for they found her more spiritual in her religious fervor. She never ceased to show greater affection for them, especially for her sister Rosa who was several years older than she. Rosa had caught a glimpse of the New Testament through Edith's example and was later drawn to the Carmelites too.

We have Edith's account of her last visit to her home in Breslau when she informed her mother that she was about to enter the convent. "My last day at home, October 12, fell on a fast day. It was the end of the Feast of the Tabernacles for the Jews. It was also my birthday. I accompanied my mother to the synagogue. We wanted to spend the day in the greatest possible intimacy. The Rabbi gave a fine sermon. On the way there we had taken the tram and spoke little. Now Mama wanted to walk home. You had to count on at least a forty-five minute walk, and she was already eight-four years old! To console her a little, I told her that my first months in the convent would be a trial period. But she replied,

" 'If you have decided to make a trial of this life, you intend to persevere.' Then she asked me, 'Wasn't it a beautiful sermon?'

" 'Yes indeed.'

" 'One can, therefore, be pious while remaining a Jew?'

" 'Certainly, if one does not know anything more.'

" 'Why did you have to learn something more?' she asked in despair, and added, 'I have nothing against Him. . . . It is possible that He was a very good man. But why did He make Himself God?'

"After lunch, she went to the store as was her custom, but soon she came back in order to stay with me. Ordinarily, she would have spent the day there.

"Many of our relatives and near-relations came with their children during the afternoon, as well as a few of my friends. It was better to have company; it created a diversion. However, as one after the other left, the family atmosphere became heavy. At the end, Mama and I were left alone in the room. My sisters were busy cleaning up and doing the dishes. She sat down then, placed her head between her hands and began to weep. I slid behind her chair and, taking that precious head with its white hair between my hands, I pressed it against my heart. . . . We remained thus for a long time, until it was time to retire. I took Mama to her room and, for the first time in my life, helped her to undress. Then I sat on her bed. . . . Finally, she sent me to rest. Neither of us slept that night.

"My train was to leave at eight o'clock. Elsa and Rosa accompanied me. Erna also would have liked to come, but I asked her to stay at the house with Mama. I knew that of my sisters she was the one who was able to console her best. Erna and I were the youngest. We had kept our habits of childlike tenderness with Mama. . . . The older ones no longer ventured to do so although their affection was no less than ours.

"At five-thirty I went, as usual, to the first Mass. Then we found ourselves around the breakfast table. Erna arrived at seven o'clock. Mama tried to eat something, but she soon pushed her cup away and began to weep as she had done the day before. I came over to her and held her close until it was time to leave. Then I motioned to Erna to take my place while I went to put on my coat and hat in an adjoining room. At last came the good-byes.

"Mama embraced me tenderly. Erna thanked me for having helped her in her work and said to me, 'May the Eternal One be with you.' Just as I embraced Erna, Mama began to weep aloud. I went out quickly accompanied by Rosa and Elsa. No one leaned out of the window to wave to me as was our custom. . . ."

Nevertheless, Edith Stein went on her way to Cologne and the convent there, not with death in her soul but carrying her sacrifice as an offering to God. Two and a half years after she had received the Carmelite habit, on September 14, 1936, when, as Sister Teresa Benedicta she was renewing her religious vows, old Mrs. Stein died at the age of eighty-eight after prolonged suffering attributed to a cancer of the stomach. A friend of the family in order to console her expressed the view that Mrs. Stein had perhaps been converted shortly before her death, but Sister Benedicta replied in the words I have already quoted:

"The unwavering faith which sustained her entire life did not fail her at the moment of death. I believe that this faith permitted her to triumph over the torments of agony and earned for her the treasures of mercy of a judge with whom she is now my most faithful support. May her intercession help me to reach my goal."

After weeks of silence her mother had begun to write to her, and shortly before her death she had sent Edith an affectionate card. She died, fortunately, before Hitler's barbaric persecutions of the Jews, or, at least, before his bloody decrees. She would have feared for her daughters, Edith and Rosa, for Rosa, who had long wanted to enter the Catholic Church but had delayed in order to care for her mother during her last illness, went at last to Cologne and was baptized in the chapel of the Carmelites. Soon afterward she followed her sister's example and entered the convent. Another sister, Erna Stein, fearing Hitler's threats, left Breslau and embarked for the United States with her entire family.

When Edith and Rosa were arrested, Edith had less confidence in the humanity of her persecutors than Rosa did. A witness relates that in the camp at Amersfort at the moment of the departure of the deportees for the concentration camp at Auschwitz, she was astonished by Sister Benedicta's demeanor. "She hardly spoke at all and looked at her sister Rosa with inexpressible sadness. Doubtless she foresaw the fate of all of them."

What happened in my own family also affords proof that the life of the cloister does not alter family love. From Savoy I took my sister, Valentine, who was tormented by a religious vocation to the novitiate of the Daughters of Charity at Paris. The moment she got onto the train she went to the open window and remained there as long as she could distinguish the little group on the platform who were waving good-by. Then she sat down and the barrier she had built up against her sorrow so as not to sadden our mother was let down. I took her hand and we remained thus for a long time. What could one say to console her? At such a moment words fail.

We spent the night in the coach. In the morning before we arrived at Paris she wept a little more. In order to cheer her up I assured her that if she could not stand this change of life and became homesick for her family and native countryside, I would immediately come to bring her home. Nothing was definite yet. She did not have to stifle her feelings.

"Oh, it isn't that," she replied. "I believe in my vocation, in the call from God. I resisted Him for such a long time. But perhaps never to see Mother again, that is hard, you know."

Upon our arrival in Paris I offered to show my sister the city. "Just Notre Dame," was her request. Then we went along the embankment of the Seine to the mother house on the Rue du Bac. We were received by an old Sister, a sort of Cerberus, who demanded of us in a rather cross voice, "What do you want?" It was not a very encouraging welcome. However, when I explained the reason for our coming, the Sister immediately softened and led us into the parlor. There as we were waiting, Valentine threw her arms around my neck and began to sob. At this moment I represented to her the whole family, and as she was about to lose this last tie, she realized all of its delicate strength.

A nun led us upstairs to the superior. We must have presented a touching spectacle. Valentine was overcome by emotion, and I was in rather a bad way. The superior gave us a little speech full of celestial allusions, no doubt very well put, but she would have done better had she simply embraced the new novice.

After this rather cool reception I had the happy thought of asking for Sister Louise Bincaz, a sister of one of my friends from the same part of France who had entered the religious life a few years before and who was employed, because of her intelligence, in administrative work. She came running in, embraced my sister with all her heart, and made the first move to sympathize with her in the pain of leaving home.

"When I left Mama," she said to us almost laughingly, "all I thought about was bringing a dozen handkerchiefs because I foresaw that I would cry a lot. And I certainly did. I used up the dozen that way."

After a few years in Paris where she took care of little children, my sister requested that she be sent to the Missions. My mother wrote to me about it, saying in substance: "Three months ago Valentine begged me to lend my support to a request she was making to her superiors asking to go to Madagascar or to China. I told her that she should leave it to her superiors and promised for my part to abandon all my rights to the superior general 'to send you,' I said, 'wherever she judges you would be most useful and could do the most good.' From then on I could do nothing more. Perhaps it is best that way. . . . When a soul has made the resolution to abandon all things in order to serve God, it is best that it always continue to make progress in the way of renunciation."

I have never forgotten this sentence. Valentine left for China. There she learned of the death of our mother, and it was she who consoled us by her ardent faith in eternal reunion. She had

ducted with extreme precision and rigor to reach the truth. Now, after twenty-five years of reflection, Bergson had found God, or if you prefer, God had found him. Thus he was, as I told him, on the threshold of Christianity. 'Much more than on the threshold,' he corrected me. But he still had to take the step, and it was meeting Father Pouget which made it possible for him to do so."

It is on this point that I venture to deviate from Jacques Chevalier's version. For Father Pouget did not obtain from Bergson his formal adhesion nor, moreover, did he ask for it. Bergson's attitude toward Catholicism was one of desire bordering on affirmation. When I saw him at Aix-les-Bains at the end of August, 1939, he foresaw the declaration of war and the evils which were about to swoop down upon mankind "whose body," in his own words, "had increased beyond measure at the expense of its soul."

A Carmelite nun wrote to Chevalier about Bergson as follows. "What I find particularly beautiful in Bergson is the intellectual *purity* of his doctrine and of his entire work. Is there not a simple and sovereign rectitude in the order of ideas just as there exists a higher purity in the order of feelings and acts? I was deeply moved by his desire, so direct and passionate, for truth and by the purity of the means which he employed in his search. . . . We cannot approach such souls without being benefited."

Jacques Chevalier describes Bergson's state of soul thus: "Turning his attention to history of which he had always been fond, Bergson concluded that with the coming of the Gospel there was a complete break, the commencement of a new world. Christianity resulted from this New Dispensation, and its diffusion throughout the civilized world brought about a renovation of the human soul. 'Not that I believe that human nature is changeable,' he told me, 'for the longer I live, the more pessimistic I become about mankind sunk as it is in the interests, vanity and envy which beget hatred and war. But human nature has been tamed by Christianity, which alone can save it, if indeed it can be saved, if it can escape the forces of evil, those diabolic forces that take advantage of the least failing of our will in order to achieve their work of destruction.' "

In a speech delivered at Evreux, Bergson also said that, "Whereas through the mind we see God here below only in enigma, or in a mirror, through the heart we can attach ourselves to Him in a love which will achieve the perfection of an unchangeable steadfastness in glory."

It is through Jesus Christ, the Saviour and Redeemer of the world that we have access to this God who is the Creator of things visible and invisible and whose power and magnificence we can only glimpse. Toward the end of his life Henri Bergson did come to the Catholic faith, at which time he must have received the baptism of desire, but he did not ask for the purifying waters of baptism. He was dissuaded by his associates who brought up, exactly as did the friends and relatives of Edith Stein, the matter of the persecution of the Jews. In contrast to the Carmelite who envisaged her conversion to the religion of Christ and her love for the Jewish people as on two different planes, Bergson allowed himself to be persuaded, or rather he hesitated. Yet he did not really hesitate if we are to believe his will in which he states:

"My reflections have led me closer and closer to Catholicism in which I see the complete fulfillment of Judaism. I would have been converted if for a number of years I had not seen in process of preparation (to a large extent, alas, through the fault of a certain number of Jews entirely lacking in moral sense) the formidable wave of Anti-Semitism which is about to break upon the world. I wanted to remain among those who tomorrow will be persecuted. But I hope that a Catholic priest will be willing, provided the Cardinal Archbishop of Paris grants permission, to come to say the prayers at my funeral. In the event that it should be necessary, call a rabbi, but do not hide from anyone my moral adhesion to Catholicism as well as the desire I have expressed first to have the prayers of a Catholic priest."

The will was dated February 8, 1937 and Bergson died January 3, 1941. His wish was granted and a Catholic priest, Canon Lelièvre of Neuilly came to say the prayers at his burial.

And nevertheless the humble Carmelite was right rather than the illustrious philosopher. Her conversion to the Catholic religion was on another plane than that of her love for the Jewish people and the desire to unite herself with them in their persecution. For proof I need only refer to the protest made on July 11, 1942 by the Catholic bishops of Holland together with the synod of the Reformed Church against the decrees of Hitler. These decrees ordered that every Jewish child be expelled from the schools and that citizens of Jewish origin be prohibited from holding public office — in short, the Jewish people were banished from society. No distinction was made between Jews converted to Catholicism or to Protestantism and those who remained faithful to the religion of the Talmud. Hitler's decrees went much further, however, extending to deportation, to the concentration camps, the gas chambers and the crematory ovens.

Arrested by the Gestapo on August 2, 1942 at the Carmelite Convent of Echt, Edith and her sister Rosa underwent all sorts of vexations before their arrival at the barracks in Amersfort. There the S.S. soldiers with their rifle butts forced them into the dormitories where they were locked up without having been given anything to eat. Let us remember this well. The non-Catholic Jews had received some food. Consequently, the Catholic Jews were treated more severely than the others. Sister Benedicta atoned even to martyrdom for the sins of Israel.

She left for Auschwitz in Silesia, the last halting place on the way to martyrdom. The religious among the prisoners formed a sort of little community. There were several Trappistines, a Dominican, and the Carmelites, Edith and Rosa Stein. Sister Benedicta comforted the others by the rare words of eternal hope which came forth from the depths of her silence. "What distinguished her from the other religious," writes Mrs. Bromberg, who escaped the holocaust, "was her silence. I had the impression that she was sorrowful to the very depths of her soul, but not in anguish. I do not know how to express it, but the weight of her suffering seemed immense, crushing, with the result that when she smiled, her smile came from such a depth of suffering that it hurt. . . ." She suffered for her people who did not know the cross of the Saviour.

Concerning her interior life I should like to quote from her writings the following passage which gives an inkling of the intensity of her prayer. "It is in secrecy and silence that the work of the Redemption is accomplished. The living stones which serve in the building of the Kingdom of God, the instruments that He chooses, are formed and polished in the silent dialogue between the soul and Him. The torrent of mystical graces which flows through the ages is the deepest and the main part of the Church's river of prayers and not merely a branch deviating from it. If this torrent causes well-established forms to give way, it is because it is animated by the Holy Spirit who breathes where He wills and who, having created all forms, reserves the right to continue making new ones. Without this Spirit there would exist neither Liturgy nor Church.

"The soul of David, the royal psalmist, vibrated like a harp under the delicate touch of the Holy Spirit. From the overflowing heart of the Virgin full of grace sprang the *Magnificat*. The canticle of the *Benedictus* opened the mute lips of old Zachary when the secret word of the angel became a visible reality. What rose from those hearts filled with the Holy Spirit expressed itself in word and action and is transmitted from mouth to mouth. It is for the Divine Office to enable the message to pass on from generation to generation.

"These many voices will dissolve and be lost in the immense current of the mystical river whose sonorous rumble rises like a great canticle of praise to the Holy Trinity — God the Creator, the Redeemer, the Vivifier. And that is why it would be false to separate or oppose the two forms of prayer — personal prayer which is called *subjective* and social or liturgical prayer which is called *objective*.

"Every true prayer is a prayer of the Church. . . . What is the prayer of the Church, then, if not the gift of the Spirit of Love to God who is Love?"

Edith Stein does not separate objective prayer from personal prayer. She prays for her family, for the Jewish race from which she came, for Christians universally, and for all men, including her executioners. She goes far beyond all those philosophers who are on the brink of faith but who refuse to pray. Her conversion took her all the way to Carmel, yet it did not take away her heart which, on the contrary, became more and more filled with love in God.

Chapter 7

UNIVERSAL
LOVE

After completing her major work, *Finite and Eternal Being,* which was an inquiry into the meaning of being and in which she started from created things in order to ascend to their divine exemplar, Edith Stein wrote a little biography of St. Teresa of Avila. Then she set herself to work in her Carmelite cell on a study of St. John of the Cross whom she had taken as a model. This work, *The Science of the Cross,* would have been her masterpiece but she was prevented from completing it by her deportation and death.

Following the example of St. John of the Cross, Sister Benedicta mounted from the love of family and race to universal love. She herself noted this ascent. "It is certain that whoever visits the Lord in his House will not always speak to Him about himself nor about his petty preoccupations, but will begin to interest himself in the concerns of the Saviour. Daily participation in the Sacrifice of the Mass draws us without our realizing it into the great current of the liturgical life. The prayer of the Church and the example of the saints penetrate the soul more and more deeply. The offering of the Holy Sacrifice renews it and brings it back to the essential mystery of our faith, the corner-stone which bears the world — the Redemptive Incarnation."

Sister Rosa-Pia, who was also a Carmelite, tells us that on

August 2, 1942, the day that Sister Benedicta was arrested, she was still working on her manuscript. "She used to leave her cell a little before the bell to go down for Matins, for she often got up ahead of time in the morning. Through the open window she could be seen silently praying with her arms extended like a cross. Sister Benedicta and her sister Rosa spent long hours every day praying in this manner. They were probably impelled to do so not only to satisfy their own personal longing but also to intercede before God as Esther and Judith had done long before. They prayed with an intense love in order to disarm Divine Justice and obtain mercy for the victims and for their executioners. . . ."

Dom Daniel Feuling, O.S.B., of Beuron Abbey, who saw her at the Carmel in Cologne, describes Sister Benedicta in the unfolding of her interior life. "I was in the presence of a soul which had surrendered itself completely to God. If the first aim of the great Teresa of Avila was to lead her daughters by way of contemplation to the mystical life and to union with God, then I dare assert that Sister Benedicta walked in this path with firm step. She seemed completely at ease in her life with the Carmelites, and I was impressed by the accent of sincerity and joy with which she expressed her happiness at having become a Carmelite. When I took leave of her, I did so with the joyous conviction that she had done well to aim so high and to choose a strictly cloistered life in order to be more intimately united to God through the bond of vows. I am convinced that she never ceased to grow. When she was forced to leave the Carmelites at Cologne to take refuge in another convent, and when the wickedness of men and their hatred of God dragged her from the silence of the cloister in order to make her climb the long path to an obscure and sorrowful Calvary, she was more than ever fulfilling her vocation. God in His loving design must have wished to conform her in this way to the ideal towards which she was striving with all the strength of her being, making of her a genuine spouse, totally consecrated, truly a Carmelite."

She followed St. John of the Cross and discovered in him the poet and the mystic. Poetry and theology, adoration and mysticism are intertwined in his work like two gillyflowers, growing close together on a church wall above which they rise balancing themselves in the blue sky like a single flower. His treatises are paraphrases of his poems and give us the key to them. With this key one can open the tabernacle in which reposes the ciborium containing the Sacred Species.

Elisabeth de Miribel in her biography of Edith Stein gives us the following analysis of her book, *The Science of the Cross*.

"In a short preface Edith Stein sets forth a plan which is not without boldness. In the light of her experiences as a Carmelite she enters as though by divination into the heart of the teachings of St. John of the Cross and endeavors to show the unity of his doctrine, even carrying it to a higher degree of clarity by appealing to the contributions of modern research on the philosophy of the person, and by introducing into his vocabulary some terms foreign to the holy doctor, such as the *self*, *liberty*, and *person*.

"The Introduction treats the meaning of the science of the Cross and its original foundation. It is in Saint John of the Cross that Edith Stein seeks such a science. 'Here,' she tells us, 'science is not spoken of in its ordinary sense. We do not have in mind a pure theory, a collection of true propositions considered as such, or an ideal edifice constructed by thought. We have in mind, certainly, a known truth, a theology of the Cross, but it is a living, existential and fruitful truth, resembling a seed cast into the soul. . . . It is this kind of theoretical exposition that we find in the doctrine of Saint John of the Cross. We shall try to discover in his writings and in his life what gives them their unity and special character.'

"The book is divided into three parts. The first is entitled *The Message of the Cross*. In it the author describes the sequence of graces by means of which Christ drew Saint John of the Cross progressively into the depths of the mystery of the Cross. This part ends with an important quotation from *The Ascent of Mount Carmel,* concerning the necessity of entering through the narrow door. This is the content of the message of the Cross.

"The second part, which is the most important, studies the doctrine of the Cross. The relation between the Cross and the night (*The Dark Night of the Senses*), is closely examined as well as the relation between the soul and faith which is the relation of death to spiritual resurrection (*The Dark Night of the Spirit*), and of the spiritual marriage of the soul (*The Living Flame of Love* and *The Spiritual Canticle*).

"The third part is entitled *The School of the Cross.* It is a fragment of some forty pages in which the author assembles passages from the holy doctor and testimonies from his contemporaries, and then gives an account of his death, borrowing from documents collected by Father Bruno de Jesus-Marie. It is here that the manuscript stops, and it remained unfinished. For just as Newman did not write the final part of his book, *The Development of Doctrine,* but lived it by entering the Church, so Edith Stein did not complete her book, *The Science of the Cross,* but lived it intensely by dying for the Cross. . . ."

In what literary form are we to seek the thought of St. John of the Cross? Surely in his hymn of love, for *The Dark Night* like *The Spiritual Canticle,* and *The Ascent of Mount Carmel* like *The Living Flame* are nothing save hymns of divine love.

This little man of Fontiveros, who came of the impoverished gentry, had mingled with the common people and the tradesmen, the weavers and the blacksmiths, the ironworkers and the silkweavers. How could he have failed to absorb the folk songs and ballads which he heard at the fairs of Medina del Campo, in the workshops, on the highways, and around the water springs? How could he have failed to blend them with religious motets, hymns, and liturgical songs? His musical ear retained their quantity and measure. Later, as a student at Salamanca, he discovered in the Bible the great rhythms and the sublime imagery which give to the language of the prophets its incomparable tonality and richness. He became enraptured with the psalms of David whose harp strings still vibrate, and by the verses of Ezechiel, the lamentations of Jeremias, and by the burning ardor of the *Canticle of Canticles*.

When inspiration seized him, whether in the monastery at Duruelo, the prison at Toledo, or in gentle Andulusia, and when he wished to express what he felt, verse came naturally to his lips. He did not search for any learned form. He was satisfied with the simplest music, that of the plaintive ballads he had heard as a boy in which the same refrain is repeated over and over and each verse finishes with the same vocables and the impact of the same assonance. Such stanzas become easily fixed in the memory. They accompany the monk in his meditation, the mother rocking her child, the young girl at her sewing, the religious seeking words for her adoration. They become a spiritual exercise.

And so it is that without their author having intended it, his verses are possessed of a highly scientific rigor and take their place with the most refined poetry. The imagery inspired by natural beauty and reinforced by recollections of the Old and New Testaments composes a kind of landscape in which the planes seem to be confused in an excess of light, in a sort of halo of golden dust which dispels the shadows and replaces them with nearly blinding rays. From this point on it is evident that the poet, as well as the mystic, has encountered the inexpressible. Human language can offer him only common syllables, sentences arranged in the order used by mortals in their daily existence. Even amplified and magnified by the artists of the Word, this language remains powerless to translate the ecstasies which the feeling of God's presence evokes in him — the presence of God in nature, in the least blade of grass as in the nocturnal song of the stars, in the weakest of beings as in the greatest genius, the presence of God outside of oneself and within, the communion with Him in a supreme ascent.

How can this converse between the creature and the Creator,

this elevation of the soul lost in the glory of the Most High ever be conveyed? And yet must we not attempt to convey something of these flights and these joys? Is it not an obligation to distribute one's riches to the poor, and what treasures can be compared to this divine bliss?

St. John of the Cross himself more than once deplored this insufficiency. "It is a question of things so interior and spiritual," he writes to Doña Ana de Peñalosa, who had entreated him to write *The Living Flame*, "that it seems to go beyond the resources of human language."

In the prologue of *The Spiritual Canticle* he says, "For who can write down that which He reveals to [the] loving souls in whom He dwells? Who can set forth in words that which He makes them to feel? And lastly who can express that which He makes them to desire? Of a surety, no one, nay indeed, not the very souls through whom He passes. And it is for this reason that they prefer to express something of what they feel by means of figures, similitudes, and symbols, or to pour out mystical secrets rather than to employ rational explanations. To those who read them without possessing the simplicity of the spirit of love and understanding which they embody, such symbols appear to be nonsense rather than expressions of reason. An example of this may be found in the divine songs of Solomon and in other works of Holy Scripture. Since the Holy Spirit cannot express the fullness of His meaning in current and ordinary terms, He speaks a mystical language employing strange figures and similitudes."

Preserving in the words of love their fullness, loving God through faith without understanding Him — that is the explanation of the mystical poems of St. John of the Cross. Of necessity he makes use of words which have served and do serve for human love, but he enlarges their meaning until they vibrate with infinity. He employs, as does the *Canticle of Canticles*, a vocabulary of imagery and symbols drawn from the rapture of human desire, but he transfigures it and consumes its carnal ap-

pearance in a burning bush. His obscurity is but a projection
of the divine clarity whose brilliance it is impossible to sustain
and not an artistic quest, nor an impotence of the mind. The
air remains limpid and transparent.

The first ecstasy which St. Teresa experienced came about
while she was listening to a song being sung by a young Sister
to the accompaniment of a tambourine, at the moment when
there suddenly rang out the name of Jesus, which she could
never hear without being transported with joy. The same phenomenon occurred in the life of St. John of the Cross, after he
had left the prison at Toledo and gone to the Carmelite *desert*
of Calvary in the valley of the Guadalquivir. There in the
parlor of the Carmel two Sisters sang for him a song about the
suffering willed by God, and, like the seraphic virgin Mother
Teresa, he swooned away. Is it not also related that one day
Newton had to suspend his calculations simply because he
glanced up and beheld the spectacle presented by nature, and
that he began to sing a hymn to the glory of the Creator thus
revealed in His works? In order to taste the mysterious beauty of
the lyric poetry of St. John of the Cross it is necessary that one's
sensibility be open to this divine manifestation.

The poetry and mysticism of St. John of the Cross are dedicated not only to a personal God, but to His sensible presence,
perceptible to each of us. This presence animates the entire
world created for man. The positivist Vacherot, a contemporary
of Renan, pontificated: "The world is not distinct from God.
It lives and develops in the immensity of space and in the
eternity of time. It suffices to itself for its existence and its or-
ganization and has no need of a principle superior to it." Rather,
the world is not separate from God because it depends upon
Him. In this regard, the mystic's view is the very opposite of
that of the pantheist.

At the Carmel of Calvary when St. John of the Cross in
quest of solitude climbs the winding path up the hill above the
Guadalquivir, what is he seeking? Or at Granada when he leaves

the Carmel of the Martyrs in order to behold the arid and gentle country of Andalusia bounded by the snowy summits of the Sierra Nevada, whether it be in the morning hours or at nightfall when silence is purer and the air more transparent, what is he hoping to find? Is it not the presence of God dwelling in the beauty of the landscape caressed by the light of day, as well as in the slow and regular movement of the stars in the sky? His ecstasy before nature reveals to him that "God is not given to him beyond things, but God and things are given to him simultaneously."

Who of us has not known this call? And how can I forget, for my part, those nights in the mountains when from the doorway of my cabin I felt myself (in the words of the young American poet, Alan Seeger, who was killed in France during World War I) *in comradeship* with the neighboring stars whose pale rays caressed the dead world of the glaciers?

And nevertheless this contemplation is as nothing compared to the drama which will unfold itself between the soul and its Lord and Master. The soul must first pass through a double tunnel before reaching the divine light. This is the *dark night* of the senses and of the soul in which the soul laments in solitude, thinking itself abandoned,

> Where did you hide yourself,
> My beloved, leaving me full of woe?
>
> You fled like a stag,
> Leaving me wounded,
> And I went crying after you
> But you had already gone. . . .

In the dark night of the senses the soul can nowhere find consolation. No earthly good satisfies it. It knows what is lacking and seeks it in vain, while temptations multiply to hold it back and prevent it from breaking the bonds which attach it to the things of this world. Let it resist them, let it triumph over its dryness and aridity, and its liberation will begin. The purification of the soul takes place during the second Night. This is the second tunnel, longer and darker than the first, for pride, doubt, anxiety, and scruples lie in ambush here. The soul does not venture into this tunnel without fear and trembling, for it is about to accomplish the work of detachment which will deliver it finally, naked and pure, to its only love. *The Ascent of Mount Carmel,* which concludes *The Dark Night,* reveals the means for detaching oneself from all things.

> In order to arrive at knowing everything,
> Desire to know nothing.

> In order to arrive at having pleasure in everything,
> Desire to have pleasure in nothing.

> In order to arrive at possessing everything,
> Desire to possess nothing.

> In order to arrive at being everything,
> Desire to be nothing.

And also,

> When thou thinkest upon anything,
> Thou ceasest to cast thyself upon the All.

> For, in order to pass from the all to the All,
> Thou hast to deny thyself wholly in all.

> And when thou cometh to possess it wholly,
> Thou must possess it without desiring anything.

> For if thou wilt have anything in all,
> Thou hast not thy treasure purely in God.*

Desire nothing — that is, not glory, nor security, nor consolation, nor knowledge, nor taste, nor liberty, nor honor. The All — that is, the Love which leads to God in whom everything is contained. "To love," says St. John of the Cross finally, indicating the light beyond the dark night, "is to cast off for the sake of God everything which is not God." It is a return to the

---

* From *The Complete Works of St. John of the Cross,* translated and edited by E. Allison Peers (Newman Press: 1949), Vol. I, pp. 62–63.

Beatitudes: "Blessed are the pure of heart, for they shall see God." This total renunciation is reached only through faith which will be transfigured into love. Then will come the divine union sung in *The Spiritual Canticle* and in *The Living Flame of Love,* works which exhale the oriental breath of *The Canticle of Canticles.*

The soul no longer lives, but it is Christ who lives in it. "And I shall be yourself in your beauty and you shall be myself in your beauty." In short, it participates in the will of God, it loses itself in Him. And it even catches a glimpse of the mystery of the Holy Trinity in which the Father, the Son, and the Holy Spirit are one. This is the supreme ascent. In order to achieve it, the soul needs but to shed its earthly cloak.

The Seraphic Virgin composed a famous poem in which she exclaimed, *"Que muero porque no muero"* (I die because I do not die) and this theme was taken up again by St. John of the Cross in his *Verse of a Soul that Longs to See God.*

> I live without living in myself,
> And in such manner I wait,
> That I die because I do not die.

The last line is repeated as a refrain at the end of each verse. *The Spiritual Canticle* is undoubtedly the flower of the lyrical and mystical works of the poet. He is inspired by the Bible, and the languishings of the loving spouse recall those of *The Canticle of Canticles,* but with the oriental imagery he has mingled that of the arid landscapes of Castile and the gentle ones of Andalusia. The entire poem reflects the impulse and the intoxication of love. Inspired and overwhelmed by this divine love, St. John of the Cross and St. Teresa both received from it strength and zeal for their ministry, their teaching, their apostolate. They had consented to lose everything in order to gain everything, for lost in God, they possessed the wellspring of life.

This wellspring of life is full to overflowing in the lyric poetry of St. John of the Cross. Whereas today man has made himself the center of the universe, this poet comes to remind us that everything which does not bring us to a knowledge of God, in reality causes us to know nothing. Now, it is love which leads us to knowledge, and love is hindered by material obligations as well as by intellectual errors. We must liberate ourselves from both if we wish to set aside all the obstacles which prevent God from acting upon our souls and possessing them. Men hate each other only because they hate God or because they ignore Him.

Chapter 8

THE SCIENCE OF
THE CROSS

I have no information concerning the mystical flights of Edith Stein, the Carmelite Sister Teresa Benedicta. Sooner or later testimonies will reveal something of them. The prioress of the Carmelites at Cologne in her biography of Edith Stein makes a veiled allusion to the matter, and in the Introduction to the last book she wrote, *The Science of the Cross,* which was not completed because the German executioners arrested her and sent her to martyrdom, Edith Stein said, "Where there is a living faith, the teaching and the wonders of God are the center of life. Everything else is no longer important. . . ."

From a long American novel which greatly attracted me, *The Cardinal** by Henry Morton Robinson, I am borrowing these lines on the mystical state which came from the lips of a holy bishop of Rome.

"At first, all is warmth and light. The soul, rejoicing in its loverlike kinship with God, traverses a luxuriant, flowering terrain. Suddenly the landscape changes, becomes an arid desert. God's presence is withdrawn. A sense of bereavement and emptiness assails the heart. Joy turns to dust, the salt of prayer loses its savor. It is indeed the dark night of the soul. Such is the classical pattern repeated over and over again in the lives of every great mystic — and every priest. A truly illuminated soul

* New York: Simon and Schuster, 1950.

persists in its search, but the weak and malformed spirit, overcome by world-weariness and corporal disgust, sinks into
despair."

Then, quite unexpectedly, the author refers to Baudelaire.
"Consider the case of Baudelaire, an imperfect mystic whose
fastidious senses, outraged by appearances of ugliness and decay,
deceived him into morbid self-loathing. Few poets have ever
been more talented — or more pitiful. It is as though our Lord,
having fallen for the first time, had permitted Himself to be
overcome by the futility of His travail, and never risen again to
bear His cross." But the light is interior, as St. John of the
Cross, having come out of the night, tells us, and it consumes
the soul. Perfect love is this communion of life which leads us
to cherish God not as a help, or a reward, or an expiatory victim,
but as an infinite good in itself. Such was the mystical love of
St. Bonaventure, of St. Teresa, and of St. Bernard.

In *The Divine Comedy* Dante's love for Beatrice finds its
fulfillment in a dazzling vision of light in which Beatrice appears
to him as a petal of the Eternal Rose. And Dante who desired
her and loved her all his life exclaimed:

> By the all powerful love
> You drew me from servitude and you made me free.
> May your pure splendor dwell in me,
> In order that my soul, freed from desire,
> May, thanks to you, be detached from my body!

The mysticism which can give rise to such flights in an elite
called to God is not necessarily separated from ordinary life but,
on the contrary, can fructify it daily. It would be a serious error
to believe that it is reserved for the chosen few when, in fact,
it is offered to all.

The story is told of the death of a simple lay brother, Brother
Albert of the Virgin, doorkeeper of the Carmel of the Martyrs
at Granada. "His face was aglow and shone with a celestial
brightness which rendered it so marvelously beautiful that all
were in a transport of delight and poured out silent tears of

consolation. Suddenly Brother Albert exclaimed in a firm voice, 'Ah! I have seen it,' and immediately he crossed his arms on his breast. As he was already beginning to close his eyes, our venerable Father John of the Cross hastened to ask him this question, 'Brother Albert, what have you seen?' He replied, 'Love, love,' and he remained in ecstasy. . . ." Merely by opening and closing the door of the monastery this vigilant doorkeeper had achieved the interior perfection of total detachment which brought him to the love of God.

I myself was witness to a similar case, that of a peasant woman who had borne her cross in bringing up eight children, the last one of which was not yet two weeks old when she lost her husband in an accident. I can still see Julienne whom I depicted in *The Homeland*. I was present at her deathbed. Her emaciated face was almost fleshless and the skin, nearly pierced by the bones beneath it, was gradually taking on the tone of yellow wax or of old ivory, brightened by two small red spots on her cheekbones. Her faded neck was deeply furrowed. Her right hand, sinewy and dried up like a dead branch, lay extended on the bed. But in her eyes there was an expression of divine peace. Seventy-five years of work and of faith were present in that serene look. She knew that she was soon to leave this world but she was not disturbed about it.

"It requires more courage to live than to die," she declared simply.

Since it would have been difficult to hide from her the fact that she was dying, I said to her, "You will go to Paradise, my good Julienne."

Then she answered me, her eyes shining, "Paradise! So that is where you want me to go." And with a touch of mischief she added, "Do you know what I shall find there? A good armchair to sit in. I always knelt to pray, but I never sat down. . . ."

At last she found rest.

From the mysticism of St. John of the Cross there come forth like rays of light these counsels of the practical life, so contrary to the self-sufficiency, presumption, and lack of discipline characteristic of so many young people of both the past and present. Does he not say, for example, "Always incline not to what is easiest but to what is most difficult, not to what is most pleasant but to what is least pleasant, not to what is most restful but to what is most laborious, not to what consoles, but to what afflicts, not to the greatest, but to the least . . ."?

St. Francis de Sales, who is also a doctor of the Church and the author of *The Treatise on the Love of God*, explicitly recommends that religion be not separated from the duties of one's state of life, but rather that it be allowed to fortify them. "A lawyer," he writes, "must be able to go from prayer to pleading cases, a merchant to his trading, a married woman to her marital duties and the bustle of her household with such composure that their minds will not be troubled." For true religion is recognized by the fact that it is always an agent of order and never of disorder.

St. Francis de Sales was aware of the treasures which could be embraced in the life of a poor woman forgetful of self and given to the service of God in the performance of her daily tasks. So great did he know the village woman, Pernette Boutey, to be that he could not hear of her death without shedding tears. He knew what place was reserved for her, and he knew also the place that would be occupied by the modest widow of Annecy whom he caught a glimpse of following the Blessed Sacrament. "And whereas the others were carrying large candles of white wax, she carried but a small taper which she had made. Finally, the wind extinguished it. That, however, neither brought her closer to nor further from the Blessed Sacrament. She did not fail to arrive at the church at the same time as the others."

To Mme. de Chantal, stricken in one of her dearest affections, he writes, "If God were to rob you of everything, would you not have enough in having God?" Having measured the singular strength of this elite soul, St. Francis de Sales wanted her to be "completely swallowed up in God." For him as for St. John of the Cross, St. Teresa, and St. Francis of Assisi, union with God is only consummated on the summits of human intelligence and sensibility abandoned to the divine will. "Man," he writes in his *Treatise*, "is the perfection of the universe, the soul is the perfection of man, love that of the soul, and charity that of love. That is why the love of God is the end, the perfection and the excellence of the universe." But he does not reserve it alone for the contemplatives in their monasteries.

One time, in conversation with His Eminence Cardinal Baudrillart, I compared the small number of fathers and mothers admitted among the saints with the large number of monks and cloistered nuns. He answered me in the gruff tone of voice that he was fond of using when expressing truths, "It is the monks and cloistered nuns who push their candidates. But I never preach in a convent without recalling to my listeners the hidden virtues and merits of those fathers and mothers who are, as a matter of fact, too often sacrificed. . . ."

For there are among them those who, despite the worst material and moral difficulties, willingly carry their cross with love. For example, in the seventeenth century there was Louis Dulaurens, the father of ten children, who having no money bolstered the shaken courage of his wife with these words, "Do not place your hope in man but only in God. Since you are a Christian, do not be troubled by anything but have confidence in God who is the common Father of all of us, and He will send us what we need."

Who among us in the course of his life has not felt himself suddenly edified in the presence of a saintly man or woman? Sometimes the person is one whom we have known for a long time but whose unsuspected interior glory we have only lately discovered, most often at the approach of death. From others we have an immediate revelation of sanctity in a facial expression, a word uttered without affectation, or an act spontaneously done.

Such souls rise directly toward the light. They have found

their mysticism in absolute submission, which is a form of love. But the sacrifice is perhaps greater for those who, at the call of St. Teresa and of St. John of the Cross, must abandon all promise of reputation, riches, beauty, knowledge, and philosophical or literary renown to hide themselves forever in Carmel. Without doubt they enter there in the joy of their love for the Spouse whom they have chosen. Nevertheless, what complete renunciation must this choice represent to them before it is made, in that moment when they must struggle against their tenderest attachments and their most radiant hopes! Twice I was witness to this victorious struggle.

I shall not disclose any names but would, nonetheless, like to ask pardon of the individuals about whom I am going to speak. One of them was a friend of my daughter. I met her often at social events where she was always in the limelight. She had a delicate and pure face, translucent and otherworldly, a natural elegance, and a graceful carriage which attracted people to her. She was known to be witty, musically inclined, and spoiled by wealth. I enjoyed chatting with her in a corner of the drawing room when she was not dancing or engaged with the young people, and since she smiled at everyone with an amiable and mysterious smile, I was prompted one day to say to her, "You seem to have a secret. . . ." When she came to announce her departure for the Carmelites after the death of her grandmother, whom she had taken care of until the very end (and it was this that had delayed her vocation), she turned gently towards me and added, "This was my secret." My oldest daughter went to a distant Carmelite convent to be present when she took the veil. She was very beautiful in her wedding dress, and my daughter wept upon seeing her disappear, her hair cut, behind the grill of the cloister.

The other person I met in Canada. She was the daughter of a senator from Trois-Rivières, and one of the most intelligent and best educated young women in the entire Province of Quebec. She wished to see me undertake a book which would link together as in former times the new and the old France. I was driven in her automobile through the Saint-Rémy valley above Trois-Riviéres, which was to be the setting of this Canadian novel. And then one day in France I received the letter in which she announced that she was entering the Carmelites. "If you return to this country," she wrote, "I shall not have the pleasure of driving you about and perhaps not even that of speaking with you. We are leaving tomorrow, my father and I, for Quebec where we shall attend a state luncheon in honor of our sovereigns [it was the time that the king and queen of England visited Canada]. The luncheon, which had to be delayed two days, coincides with the date set for my entrance. And so, like Madame Louise of France I shall eat at noon at the table of the king and in the evening at that of the Carmelites. . . ."

A breath from above caressed the ardent souls of these young women. They now belong to that spiritual choir which in all parts of the world compensates by its prayers for the daily accumulation of human faults and errors, and which, in the tragic time in which we live, beseeches the living God, the God of love, to put an end to the evils of war and to grant both internal and external peace to poor mankind. In all the sanctuaries of the Carmelite order lamps burn day and night. But the pure flame which rises from so many hearts burning with love — how could this not be pleasing to the Lord?

Chapter 9

MARTYRDOM

It was from one of these Carmelite sanctuaries that Sister Teresa Benedicta was dragged away to be tormented and put to death. Her own sufferings must have reminded her of those of St. John of the Cross. For having upheld the reforms of Saint Teresa he was beaten with switches in the monastery of Avila and incarcerated at Toledo by the Carmelite fathers of the mitigated rule. His prison cell opened upon the Tagus. "Toledo," writes one of his biographers, "is rugged and warm. Moorish refinements, Christian festivities, Spanish violences — nothing has satisfied its desire. It reaches beyond everything: blood, sensibility and death. Toledo, riveted to the rock, is a *cry in the desert*. Its thirst is unquenchable. It has the appetite of the sun."

I hardly dare to give the details of his martyrdom cited by his biographer, Father Bruno. ". . . The Saint of the Carmelites was then imprisoned in a narrow hollow six feet wide and ten feet long, which was used as a storage place. Air and light came only from a skylight high above him. Saint John of the Cross had to use a stool in order to get enough light to say his Office. Every evening the monks led him into the refectory (later it was only on Fridays) where he ate bread and water seated on the floor. This was the ignominious fast instituted for incorrigible faults. Then he would undress to the waist, and they would all take turns in striking him. 'Senseless block,' they would shout at

him in irritation. But he showed himself as immovable as a
stone. In the face of such steadfastness and patience the young
novices said to themselves, 'He is a saint,' and they wept."

The fathers of the mitigated rule, however, remained heart-
less and took delight in tormenting him. In vain, after having
mistreated him, would they urge him to give up his reform. He
experienced what he called the *Dark Night* when both body
and soul seem abandoned by God, but he would not weaken.
He guessed what Mother Teresa, for her part, must have been
suffering when, not knowing the place of his detention, she ap-
pealed to Philip II himself to learn the whereabouts of the
prison. Through his death to the world he knew that he would
really live again. His jailer, who was less inhuman, had pity on
him and gave him "a little paper and ink." It was in this hor-
rible prison of Toledo that John of the Cross composed his two
poems, *The Dark Night* and *The Spiritual Canticle*, or at least,
it was there that he composed them orally and committed them
to memory during the long hours of solitude and darkness.

The executioner of Sister Teresa Benedicta showed her no
charity at all in order that she might not be able to give voice
to her torture but might die in humility.

The period following Luther's Reform was one of frightful
religious conflict somewhat comparable to that of our own age
which goes from existentialism to intellectual aberration, but
also to a divine curiosity. In such times the greatest virtues and
the worst errors grow together like healthy trees and poisonous
plants in a tropical jungle — a combination of great mystics and
of *illuminati*, of theology and sorcery, of apparitions and ecstasies, of possessions and genuine demoniacal interventions. In
such a chaos of ideas and systems those who believe themselves
to be in possession of the truth seek to impose it upon the world
by all the means at their disposal, even by torture and death.
Thus is explained the Inquisition and the Massacre of Saint
Bartholomew. Thus is also explained, in part, the Resistance
with its heroisms, its errors, and its crimes. They are explained,

but they are not justified. "The more saintly confessors are," says St. John of the Cross, "the more gentle they are and the less they are scandalized." But saintliness is rare, especially among those who are in possession of power, even spiritual power, for the spirit of domination too often takes hold of them.

St. John of the Cross was completely the opposite of such pious and fearful tyrants. He drew people to himself, and he consoled them. At Granada where he built a spacious monastery with a beautiful cloister, far from rejecting the Moors, he treated them with tenderness and pity. The possessed and the *illuminati* were brought to him from everywhere. This mystic, who concealed his ecstasies because he realized the contagion that a false imitation of supernatural phenomena could spread, showed in *The Ascent of Mount Carmel* how very necessary it is in this domain to mistrust everything which is outside reason.

"We must," he writes, "attach ourselves so much to reason and to the evangelical teaching that if we should happen, either in spite of ourselves or with our own free consent, to receive some supernatural communication, we would accept of it only what was found to be in perfect conformity with both of these and would accept it not because it was revealed but because it was a reasonable thing, leaving aside what was purely revelation." Such is the teaching of this mystic, the enemy of all religious deviation.

The ministry of St. John of the Cross reconciles the hermitage and the mission, contemplation and the apostolate. Is this not the very spirit of the Carmelite Reform? And is he not in this respect the faithful continuator and disciple of St. Teresa, who died in 1582? As Vicar-Provincial of Andalusia he went to the general chapter at Madrid on June 4, 1591 for the elections. There he was deprived of his offices. Nevertheless, when the work of St. Teresa was brought into question, he rose to defend it. The Superior-General, beside himself with indignation over the protestation of a one-time provincial who was no longer anything but a simple monk, sent him off to do penance in the solitude of the Penuela in the Sierra Morena. He thought to punish John of the Cross in this way, but the saint was happy to be relieved of all administrative duties and to be able to give himself entirely to divine love. But his health was impaired. He suffered cruelly from an ulcer of the leg, and on September 21 he had to leave Penuela, hoisted upon a mule, for Ubeda where he would find medical care.

"Ubeda," says Maurice Barrès who visited the place, "is one of those poor and precious cities, those iron jewels, those ardent cries that strike hard upon the soul and caress it." But the prior of Ubeda gave a poor welcome to the sick man who had been taken to task at the general chapter, and the Father Procurator complained of the expense that he caused. For subordinates do not hesitate to add by flattery and meanness to the severity of their superiors.

In the meantime, the condition of St. John of the Cross grew worse. A chance surgeon had opened his abscesses and exposed the flesh, causing him to endure the most excruciating pain, but he took refuge from his sufferings in the Passion of Christ. On December 12 he called for the Viaticum. His gentleness and his humility were such that the prior and the procurator, who had been won over, came and wept at the bedside of the dying man. He himself followed his own agony from hour to hour and announced his end for midnight of December 13. When he expired, clutching the crucifix after having brought it to his lips for the last time, a great brightness shone over his whole body and over the litter upon which he lay.

We know nothing of the last hours of Edith Stein. For this reason it is of utmost importance that the person or persons be found who were in charge of the crematory ovens at Auschwitz in order that they may be questioned about her death. It is impossible that they did not notice a saint even though she went most naturally, most simply and most humbly to her execution; for holiness is divine. It is visible at the last moment even to the eyes of an executioner.

In the trial of the Gestapo of Marseilles, held before a military tribunal at Lyons in March of 1955, there was question of a convoy of women deported to Auschwitz, of whom about a thousand were upon their arrival put directly into the gas chambers. It is absolutely essential that the witnesses be questioned, but if no witnesses be found, then let us get down on our knees before the Carmelite Teresa Benedicta, martyr.

Dom Raphael Walzer, Abbot of Beuron, states this opinion of her, "We do not pretend to prejudge the decisions of the Church concerning her. Whether she be raised to the altar or not, one thing will forever remain true: her example, her prayer and her works, her silence and her suffering, her calm and peaceful march towards the camp of death will not escape the memory of men.

"Her testimony dispenses strength and light. It awakens in each of us a profound aspiration which draws us invincibly towards the abyss of faith, hope, and charity."

*   *   *   *

Here is the prayer recited in Catholic Germany for the canonization of Edith Stein, a prayer which was sent to me by the prioress of the Carmelites at Cologne.

O Eternal God, from whom all things take their being, we thank Thee for the great gifts and graces which Thou hast bestowed on Thy servant Teresa Benedicta of the Cross. Thou hast given these to her that she may be for us a light for learning and an example of virtue. We implore Thine infinite majesty to glorify her and allow her to be counted among the holy ones of Thy Church, for during her life she sought nothing else than to save souls through the cross of Thy Son and thus to glorify Thy name. Who livest and reignest, world without end. Amen.*

*   *   *   *

May Catholic Germany see in her the redemptress of the Hitler regime, and may the Christian world celebrate in this

---

* NOTE: The English version of this prayer was prepared by the Cologne Carmelites.

martyr, whose death was an apotheosis of prayers although it was without doubt cruel and appalling, since she was placed in the crematory oven, the symbol of all the victims of wars and revolutions in our time which in the midst of technical progress retrogresses toward barbarism!

A SELECTED BIBLIOGRAPHY
OF EDITH STEIN

Primary Sources

Stein, Edith. *Werke,* Vols. 1–3, 1950 ff. Nauwelaerts (Louvain) and Herder (Freiburg). Ed. by Dr. Lucie Gelber and Father Romaeus Leuven, O.C.D., and containing:

Kreuzeswissenschaft (Vol. 1)
Endliches und Ewiges Sein (Vol. 2)
Des hl. Thomas von Aquino Untersuchungen uber die Wahrheit (Vol. 3)

Other volumes in preparation

This Louvain edition of the writings of Edith Stein is at present the most authoritative and the most easily available edition.

The following works of Edith Stein have been translated into English:

Stein, Edith. "The Mystery of Christmas; a Meditation." *The Tablet,* Vol. 202 (Dec. 19, 1953), pp. 594–595. Also published in: *The Catholic Mind,* Vol. 53 (Dec., 1955), pp. 707–711; *America,* Vol. 96 (Dec. 22, 1956), p. 353; *Jubilee,* Vol. 4 (Dec., 1956), pp. 11–14.

Teresia Benedicta a Cruce, Sister. "Ways to Know God" (*Wege der Gotteserkenntnis*). Trans. by Rudolph Allers in *The Thomist,* Vol. 9 (July, 1946), pp. 379–420.

The Writings of Edith Stein. Selections edited and introduced by Hilda C. Graef (Westminster: Newman Press, 1956), and (London: Peter Owen Ltd., 1956).

Secondary Sources

Allers, Rudolph. Review of Edith Stein's *Endliches und Ewiges Sein* (*The Finite and the Eternal*). *The New Scholasticism,* Vol. 26 (Oct., 1952), pp. 480–485.

Baird, R.S.M., Sister Mary Julian. "Edith Stein and the Mother of God." *Cross and Crown,* Vol. 8 (Dec., 1956), pp. 417–429. Reprinted as a Marian Reprint No. 59 under the same title at the Marian Library, Dayton, Ohio.

Barrat, Robert, "Martyrdom of Edith Stein," *Commonweal*, Vol. 55 (Jan. 25, 1952), pp. 396–398.

Brackett, S.J., R. "Edith Stein's Way of the Cross," *The Catholic World*, Vol. 181 (May, 1955), p. III.

Braybrooke, N. "The Called and the Chosen," *Doctrine and Life*, Vol. 8 (July, 1958), pp. 120–125.

Candish, F. "Edith Stein (1892–1942)." *Furrow*, Vol. 4 (Sept., 1953), pp. 500–509.

Collins, James. "Edith Stein and the Advance of Phenomenology." *Thought*, Vol. 17 (Dec., 1942), pp. 685–708.

———— Review of Edith Stein's *Endliches und Ewiges Sein*. *The Modern Schoolman*, Vol. 29 (Jan., 1952), pp. 139-145.

———— "The Fate of Edith Stein," *Thought*, Vol. 18 (June, 1943), p. 384.

Conway, M. D., "Edith Stein: a Woman of Today." *Magnificat*, Vol. 95 (Oct., 1955), pp. 51–55.

De Miríbel, Elisabeth. *Edith Stein (1891–1942)*, Préface de Henri Irénée Marrou. En appendice: *Le grand oeuvre d'Edith Stein* par Aloïs Dempf (La Vigne du Carmel) (Paris: Editions du Seuil, 1954).

Devaux, André A. "Vocation in the Life and Thought of Edith Stein." *Philosophy Today*, Vol. 2, nos. 3/4 (Fall, 1958), p. 172.

Egan, M. J. *The Story of Edith Stein* (Dublin: Catholic Truth Society of Ireland, 1957), 16 pp.

Francis, Dale, "The Gestapo's Answer." *The Voice of St. Jude* (May, 1953), pp. 11–15.

Graef, Hilda C. "Edith Stein, a Carmelite Philosopher." *The Priest*, Vol. 9 (Nov., 1953), pp. 861–868.

———— "Edith Stein Contemplates the Woman of Perfection." *The Marianist*, Vol. 48 (Oct., 1957), pp. 14–19.

———— "Edith Stein, Philosopher and Carmelite." *Cross and Crown*, Vol. 4 (Dec., 1952), pp. 393–404.

———— "Edith Stein and the Nazis." *The Catholic Digest* (May, 1953), pp. 48–52 (condensed from *Cross and Crown*).

———— "Edith Stein's Vocation." *American Benedictine Review* (Winter, 1952), pp. 348–353.

———— *The Scholar and the Cross* (London, New York: Longmans Green, 1955); (Westminster, Md.: Newman Press, 1955).

———— "This is the Truth." *The Sign*, Vol. 38 (Aug., 1958), pp. 45–47.

Grant, Cecily. "Edith Stein, Philosopher, Convert, Carmelite, Victim of the Nazis." *Catholic Truth Society* (London: 1957).

Gilman, Richard. "Edith Stein." *Jubilee,* Vol. 3 (May, 1955), pp. 39–45.

Haines, A. "She Found Truth in God." *The Christian Family,* Vol. 52 (Oct., 1957), pp. 12–14.

Holzhauer, Jean. "One of Six Million." *Commonweal,* Vol. 57 (Oct. 10, 1952), pp. 21–23.

"Jewess in a Gas Chamber." *Torch,* Vol. 40 (Mar., 1956), pp. 6–8.

"Jewish Convert." *Ave Maria,* Vol. 66 (Nov. 8, 1947), p. 578.

Marshall, M. "Modern Martyr." *Mary,* Vol. 19 (Aug., 1958), pp. 51–56.

Nicholl, Donald. "The Spiritual Writings of Edith Stein." *Life of the Spirit,* Vol. 6, No. 65 (Nov., 1951), pp. 195–200.

Oesterreicher, John M. "Edith Stein on Womanhood." *Integrity,* Vol. 7 (Sept., 1953), pp. 21–28.

———— *Walls are Crumbling* (New York: The Devin-Adair Company, 1952).

Osterman, R. "Edith Stein, Witness to Paradox." *The Catholic World,* Vol. 180 (Mar., 1955), pp. 447–451.

———— "Edith Stein — Jewish Convert — Catholic Martyr," *Epistle,* Spring, 1957.

Paul, L. "Martyr for the Jews." *Homiletic and Pastoral Review,* Vol. 55 (Apr., 1955), pp. 577–583.

Przywara, Erich. "Neo-Scholasticism in Germany." *The Modern Schoolman,* Vol. 10 (May, 1933), pp. 91–92.

Roberto, Brother. *The Broken Lamp* (Dujarie: 1957).

Stern, K. "Dying and Yet We Live." *The Catholic Worker,* Vol. 23 (Sept., 1956), p. 3.

———— "Of Rare Stature." *Commonweal,* Vol. 65 (Dec. 14, 1956), pp. 293–294.

Teresia Renata de Spiritu Sancto, Sister. *Edith Stein.* Trans. by Cecily Hastings and Donald Nicholl (London and New York: Sheed and Ward, 1952).

Tomlin, E. W. F. "Edith Stein," *Blackfriars,* Vol. 36 (June, 1955), pp. 216–222.